Toward a Pragmatist Sociology

Robert G. Dunn

TOWARD A PRAGMATIST SOCIOLOGY

John Dewey and the Legacy of C. Wright Mills

TEMPLE UNIVERSITY PRESS
Philadelphia • Rome • Tokyo

TEMPLE UNIVERSITY PRESS
Philadelphia, Pennsylvania 19122
www.temple.edu/tempress

Published 2018

Library of Congress Cataloging-in-Publication Data

Names: Dunn, Robert G., author.
Title: Toward a pragmatist sociology : John Dewey and the legacy of C. Wright Mills / Robert G. Dunn.
Description: Philadelphia : Temple University Press, 2018. | Includes bibliographical references and index.
Identifiers: LCCN 2017021819| ISBN 9781439914595 (hardback : alk. paper) | ISBN 9781439914618 (e-book)
Subjects: LCSH: Social sciences. | Sociology. | Pragmatism. | Dewey, John, 1859–1952—Political and social views. | Mills, C. Wright (Charles Wright), 1916–1962—Political and social views. | BISAC: SOCIAL SCIENCE / Sociology / General. | PHILOSOPHY / Criticism. | PHILOSOPHY / Movements / Pragmatism.
Classification: LCC H61 .D88196 2018 | DDC 301.01—dc23
LC record available at https://lccn.loc.gov/2017021819

♾ The paper used in this publication meets the requirements of the American National Standard for Information Sciences—Permanence of Paper for Printed Library Materials, ANSI Z39.48-1992

Printed in the United States of America

9 8 7 6 5 4 3 2 1

Contents

Preface

Given a renewed interest in pragmatism among both philosophers and sociologists, I would expect this study to arouse a certain amount of interest among academic readers in these and related fields. The motivation for this book, however, and my enthusiasm for the ideas of John Dewey and C. Wright Mills have origins other than the attention devoted in recent years to pragmatism. This study arises from a lingering dissatisfaction with the positivist tendencies and narrow scientific preoccupations of my chosen field of study, sociology. In my view, these trends have prevailed within the disciplinary mainstream at the expense of engagement with the social and human problems engendered by modern capitalist society, problems of major concern to both Dewey and Mills, among many others.

Amid the competing influences of structural functionalism, symbolic interactionism, Marxism, and the Frankfurt School of Critical Theory, all of which shaped my intellectual development as a doctoral student at the University of California at Berkeley in the 1960s, my reading of Dewey imparted an arresting sense of his pertinence to social science. Dewey has, ever since, remained a critical voice in my thinking. Better known to sociologists, and someone many consider the "conscience" of the field, Mills put his own stamp on many of

Dewey's views and concerns, translating them into an intellectually vital and politically relevant approach to sociological inquiry. The interrelated work of Dewey and Mills, to my mind, brings to light the limitations of the discipline by projecting the outlines of a sociology devoted to "the big picture," as Mills would say. While Dewey is perhaps the most prominent and influential American thinker of the twentieth century, a man of immense intellectual range, the "radical" sociology of Mills remains a beacon of inspiration for those who believe that sociology can make a difference in the real world of social and political actors. The combined insight and vision of these thinkers offer, I believe, a renewed sense of the purpose and possibilities of a genuinely critical sociology based on the spirit and principles of pragmatism.

It is my hope that this book will contribute something of value to a continuing conversation about pragmatism and its place in American social thought and academic life. My critique of sociology and treatment of pragmatism are specifically intended, however, to show how, taken together, the work of Dewey and Mills provides an intellectual and conceptual framework for the transformation of sociology into a more substantive, comprehensive, and socially useful discipline. The result would be a sociology capable of restoring a sense of moral and political purpose to a discipline still largely beholden to positivist science and the encumbrances of professionalism. If my arguments for a pragmatist-based sociology encourage present and future generations of aspiring sociologists to think seriously and self-reflexively about this philosophy's critical potential, I shall regard this work a success. More generally, in the spirit of both Dewey and Mills, I hope this book will encourage future sociologists to regard the discipline as not only a science but also an intellectual, moral, and political enterprise.

Acknowledgments

While writing is often an isolating experience, the work of academic authors, fortunately enough, always profits from the knowledge and insights of others. Though driven by my own intellectual preoccupations, I could not have brought this book to fruition without the assistance and encouragement of the following people. Parts or all of the manuscript were read by Diane Beeson, Fred Block, Ben Brast-McKie, Elliott Currie, Troy Duster, Barbara Epstein, David Fogarty, Brian Rich, Kenneth Tucker, and Norbert Wiley. Their comments have greatly improved this work. Conversations with a number of other people have influenced my thinking about pragmatism and its significance for social theory and sociological practice. Jim Stockinger, Barrie Thorne, David Wellman, and Deborah Woo offered engaging opinions and much-needed perspective. Exchanges with Hans Sluga, and his teaching of Wittgenstein and Hegel, have provided invaluable philosophical background for my approach to this study and my interpretation of Dewey. Robert Antonio offered encouragement and assisted me in obtaining materials for the text. Finally, I thank the three anonymous reviewers for Temple University Press for their helpful comments; my former editor, Micah Kleit, for his enthusiasm for the project; and my current editor, Ryan A. Mulligan, for ushering the manuscript into production.

Toward a Pragmatist Sociology

Introduction

The current revival of interest in the philosophy of pragmatism and particularly the writings of John Dewey is a development both significant and intriguing. Since its inception pragmatism has had a strong if not always recognizable presence in American intellectual life, and Dewey, his controversial reputation notwithstanding, has been widely regarded as the leading American philosopher of the past century. Why, after years of relative dormancy, we have in recent times been witnessing renewed interest in Dewey and pragmatism is a question with any number of answers. Whichever ones we choose, it is in any case clear that given its historical, intellectual, and theoretical connections to sociology, the rebirth of pragmatism has special significance for the field.

It can plausibly be argued that the rejuvenation of pragmatism is one manifestation of the exhaustion in the late twentieth century of prevailing strains of modernist thought, in particular the foundationalism and monistic structure of Enlightenment philosophy and its conceptions of reason and democracy. On this view, it is no accident that pragmatism has reemerged from the intellectual subconscious in the context of the movement called "postmodernism," with which it shares strong antifoundationalist and antiessentialist impulses. While the classic pragmatists would take umbrage at the simplistic relativizing and antihumanist elements injected into this movement by poststructuralism, the two philosophies agree on certain basic principles. Most fundamental is a firm belief in the conditioned, variable, and provisional character of knowledge and, correspondingly, skepticism toward the notion of "Truth."

The turn to pragmatism, however, can hardly be accounted for by the popularity of postmodernism. Rather, the pragmatic turn is a response to some of the same underlying *conditions* that precipitated the postmodern movement. Most important among these has been a crisis in many of the established intellectual outlooks, narratives, and habits of thought in the American university accompanying the rise of multiculturalism, consumerism, and other cultural developments. These trends have manifested themselves in an identifiable democratization of social, cultural, and political attitudes that resonate with pragmatism's antielitist tendencies.

Debates surrounding the meaning of pragmatism and its significance are nothing new in the field of philosophy. In sociology, however, where Dewey and George Herbert Mead are considered philosophical "fathers" of the Chicago tradition of symbolic interactionism, there have been novel signs of enthusiasm for exploring American sociology's philosophical roots. Regrettably, this nascent movement has tended to focus on narrow technical readings of Dewey from within the discipline's existing theoretical and methodological perspectives and attitudes. While this kind of perspective on Dewey can be useful for the further development of theory and research, it ignores a larger and more compelling set of issues. Dewey's philosophy puts forth a view of the entire scientific enterprise that is fundamentally at odds with mainstream conceptions and practices in today's social sciences. What is most important about this philosopher is his distinctive way of thinking about and viewing the world, including, most importantly, his integrated views of the nature and role of science and his holistic conceptions of human thought and society. In short, Dewey's outlook and his understanding of science and its role in society have provocative consequences for the very meaning and purpose of sociology as a scientific discipline.

Viewed from this angle, a more promising approach to a reconsideration of pragmatism would involve a broad and critical look at the present state of sociology, with its problems and promises, and a strategy for transforming it into a different kind of discipline, one that is more socially, morally, and politically concerned and relevant. This requires that we look, preferably from a fresh perspective, at what many consider problematic trends in the discipline stemming from longstanding pressures both internal and external to the profession. The purpose of such an assessment would be to consider the ways in which aspects of pragmatism, and Dewey's thought in particular, could redress the failure of sociology to reach its full potential as a science of social and human import. Of considerable importance, this would involve positioning sociology as a discipline capable of playing an active and meaningful role in public life.

In an attempt to exemplify this kind of sociology, the present study is organized largely around the key sociological writings of C. Wright Mills. Although a whole chapter is devoted to the thought of Dewey, the book is woven with ideas that were salient in Mills's work, including his critiques of the profession and American society. Mills inherited from Dewey an abiding concern for the public role the social sciences should play as a normative science focused on societal problems, the well-being of the individual, and the moral, ethical, and political concerns of society and its members. Mills attempted to implement Dewey's goal of making the problems of *human beings* living in a modern, complexly organized, and rapidly changing society the focal point of the social sciences and of intellectual life generally.

The history of American sociology is a story that could be told in many different ways. These ways reflect not only the authors' particular goals and intents but refract their biographies, social backgrounds, ideological orientations, and intellectual and practical dispositions. Such factors have obviously shaped my view of the discipline and my skepticism toward its contributions to a truly meaningful science of human society. While the history of sociology is not my primary concern, what I attempt in this book proceeds from a critical attitude toward the discipline's overall development and present state. The condensed historical overview with which I begin focuses primarily on a set of issues related to how the discipline came to define itself over time and for what reasons. I've chosen to emphasize the unhappy consequences of sociology's search for a legitimate scientific identity. While conceding the importance of its scientific efforts, I criticize the failure of the discipline to achieve a coherent sense of purpose and relevance as a result of its single-minded search for scientific prestige.

The thesis of this book comprises two interrelated parts. The first part is largely diagnostic, briefly exploring the past and present state of the discipline, critiquing its dominant tendencies, and offering historical examples of alternatives to conventional sociological approaches. The second, "remedial," and larger part examines the possibility of a different kind of sociology predicated on the views of John Dewey and the work of C. Wright Mills. By stressing the similar intellectual and moral visions of both men, this aspect of the discussion emphasizes the contrast between an "ivory tower" conception of the discipline and a definition of sociology as a critical social science engaged, in emulation of Mills, in the practice of turning "personal problems" into "public issues."

To begin, regarding the discipline's failings, divergent and competing theoretical and methodological approaches have divided sociology into rival factions or "schools" throughout much of its history. While these divisions have in certain respects created a healthy dynamic, they have also led to overly narrow thinking, fragmentation, and false issues. As a result, the discipline has lacked coherence and a sense of common purpose.

This state of affairs is largely an outcome of persistent attempts to convert the field into a positivist science in emulation of the natural sciences. Championed by those with a highly circumscribed view of science, the push toward positivism, in which science is seen as a search for immutable laws employing the methods of natural science, has slowed the progress of the field by diverting attention from the inherently human meanings and significance of sociological concepts and analysis. It is now common knowledge that causal explanations modeled exclusively on the "hard" sciences and simple fact-gathering techniques are in and of themselves inadequate and often misleading practices for an aspiring science truly representative and worthy of its subject matter. Given the historical character and complexities of society and the intricacies of human consciousness and agency, it is doubtful that sociology will ever achieve the kind of generalizable knowledge and powers of prediction displayed by the natural sciences. Despite this reality, the assumptions and methods of positivism are still granted credibility grossly disproportionate to their usefulness for genuine sociological knowledge.

The quest for a positivist sociology has manifested itself in what is usually called "formalism." A familiar feature of philosophical and scientific thought, in the context of sociology this term bears unavoidable negative connotations, referring to the restrictions imposed on theory and research by pressures to achieve scientific rigor. Formalism is that aspect of sociology burdened by an excess of abstraction, analytical constructs, formulaic methods, and mechanistic explanations, the perfection of which is presumed to be a prerequisite of scientific respectability. While conceding the importance of abstraction, I argue that unnecessary abstraction and its various forms of baggage can only hurt a discipline that thrives on substance.

Formalist sociology, in short, is woefully disconnected from the realities of social life. At worst, formalism is both cause and effect of the myopic vision of a discipline that in its pursuit of scientific status is often more preoccupied with itself than its purported object of study. While analytical clarity and technical procedure are essential to any scientific endeavor, a glance at the mainstream of sociology over the past seventy-five years shows that, despite opposition and more promising trends, such preoccupations have exercised undue influence on the discipline.

Many share in the contention that formalism can never play more than a limited and subsidiary role in sociology, whose major purpose is to describe, explain, and understand the structure, functioning, and human significance of real societies. The generalizing and purifying functions of formalist procedures are hardly suitable for the study of a social world that is full of particulars and complexity and that is historical and evolutionary in character; in other words, an object of study that is complicated and always changing. If anything, such procedures *interfere* with the theoretical depth and empirical concreteness demanded of a science of social life that is true to its object, in the sense of grasping the realities of its subject matter in a way that is meaningful and of practical consequence.

One strategy for overcoming the constraints of formalist sociology would be to adopt a broadened conception of science. Certainly, the mere fact that society and its inhabitants occupy time and space binds them to the laws of the physical universe. Also, that we are biological creatures and still to some degree live in a natural environment means that we are to some extent bound by the forces of nature. These are perhaps among a few of the reasons why sociology has been unable to dispense entirely with lawlike propositions and positivist methods. At the same time, such methods are by themselves incapable of providing adequate explanations and understandings of social reality in its full human significance. Our conception of social science accordingly needs to include a variety of methods that capture both the human and "natural" dimensions of social life.

A related strategy of creating greater coherence of purpose and a common disciplinary vision entails a larger problem: overspecialization. The extreme division of labor in sociology stems largely from the sheer size and complexity of the field. Layered over this division of labor, however, and intensifying its negative effects, are conflicts resulting from epistemological and ideological differences over what constitutes, or should constitute, knowledge in the social sciences. In place of productive differences we often find competing theoretical factions and a consequent lack of analytical coherence across the field. This appears in endless disputes over how to bring different levels of social analysis together, which often requires a reconciliation of seemingly incompatible theoretical perspectives and frameworks. While such difficulties are to some extent reflective of the multiple levels and dimensions of social life, these disputes are often artificially created and wasteful controversies resulting from a formalist frame of mind. For seriously reflective sociologists, such a situation calls for a new mode of thinking, more deliberate and honest consideration of the nature of the subject matter and how to represent it, and a reconsideration of the goals and practices of the discipline.

The second part of the thesis of this book is a multilayered response to these problems. At the most general level, the ultimate challenge to sociological formalism is a serious rethinking of the very purpose of the discipline. Formalism is the *cause* of a disembodied and fragmented sociology but also a *symptom* of a failure to definitively answer a fundamental question: Is sociology merely a science, an endeavor aimed at "knowledge for its own sake" and the needs of special interests, or is it an enterprise destined to play a critical intellectual, social, and political role in the larger society?

The primary goal of this book is to explore a groundwork and rationale for the latter conception. I begin by examining past traditions of social criticism rooted in the intellectual and moral concerns that shaped the work of some twentieth-century social thinkers. Looking backward historically, we find two interrelated lines of scholarly descent. The first, now largely forgotten, is a critical tradition in American social thought dating from the writings of the institutional economist Thorstein Veblen. This tradition includes the popular writings of a generation of post–World War II social critics, the primary thrust of whose work found explicit and more expansive expression in the sociology of C. Wright Mills. The second, allied, tradition is the philosophy of pragmatism as brought to fruition in the work of John Dewey. Mills is the pivotal figure joining these two bodies of work.

Next, I turn to a number of continuities between Mills and Dewey that express the affinities between these traditions and that I believe are crucial for an informed critique of mainstream sociology and the development of an alternative to formalism. While the importance of pragmatism to Mills's early social-psychological writings was eventually overshadowed by his turn to classical European theory, pragmatism remained a frame for much of his thinking and informed the theoretical structure, style, and method of his work. This is evident not only in Mills's enduring focus on the Deweyan theme of problem solving, most apparent in *The Sociological Imagination,* but also in his frequent reliance on the pragmatist nomenclature of rationality, knowledge, symbols, communication, democracy, and so forth, central motifs in Dewey's philosophy. I argue that a fuller understanding and appreciation of the critical vision of Mills, a vision with a potential for transforming sociology into a more relevant field, can be attained by placing him in a comparative and contrasting relationship to Dewey's pragmatism. At the same time, I see Mills's contributions as inadequate to the task of bringing about fundamental change in the field. Rather, this task depends on a reappropriation of Dewey's own intellectual vision and philosophical and theoretical ideas.

A comparison and contrast of Dewey and Mills reveals four major convergences. First, and perhaps most obvious, is their common conviction in the importance of social scientific inquiry to resolving the human problems of society. Pragmatism for Dewey was at bottom a philosophy of problem solving, and sociology for Mills was a craftsperson's effort to grasp the relationship among personal troubles, social structures, and history. Implicit in both conceptions is a belief in the unity of theory and practice, of the interconnections between thought and human action. For Dewey, philosophy itself was a form of action, and for Mills the meaning of sociology consisted ultimately in its relevance to the rule of reason and freedom in the active shaping of social institutions and people's lives.

Second, in my treatment of 1950s social criticism and the intellectual commonalities between Dewey and Mills, I hope to show that the notion of critique inherent in both lines of descent deserves a wider hearing among sociologists. For Dewey and Mills, social science had a responsibility to inquire into societal problems for the purpose of furthering public understanding and promoting social progress. Except for small pockets of the discipline, this view of social science has been largely lost. Its retrieval presupposes that ongoing critiques of society, no matter how threatening to established interests, are an essential aspect of responsible social inquiry. What such a sociology might look like is suggested by the writings of the postwar critics and given strong foundation in the work of both Dewey and Mills.

A third and closely related convergence is the role of values in the scientific enterprise. Both Dewey and Mills saw values as integral to the conduct of science, as providing a sense of meaning and moral significance to social facts and the knowledge that comes from empirical discovery. For Dewey, intelligence and values mutually informed one another, and for Mills the meaning of sociological work was inseparable from value commitments. Both men took strong exception to the fact-value distinction, seeing it as a false dichotomy akin to the wrongful separation of theory and practice. Dewey believed it was the responsibility of science to conduct itself with the aim of preserving and promoting human values. On the one hand, Mills saw sociology as a tool for identifying and protecting cherished values, while on the other hand he thought that conscious, open reflection on one's own values were a necessary precondition of objectivity in sociological investigation. Both thinkers, in short, believed that human values were just as entrenched in scientific practice as in any other social institution.

Finally, there always remain questions of what/whose values are at stake and how we are to overcome value differences and conflicts. This is a challenging problem in diverse and complex societies. In this respect, the case of Dewey and Mills is both remarkable and encouraging. Their lives were in a real sense worlds apart, Dewey coming from a rural nineteenth-century New England background steeped in an ethos of tradition, gentility, and spirituality, and Mills, a native of Texas, coming of age much later in the atmosphere and culture of the open spaces of the American West, with its legacy of frontier independence. It is thus perhaps surprising that both men developed such similar intellectual and political values and inclinations. This was evident in their social criticism and progressive politics, which manifested itself in a strong commitment to social change based on the ideals of democracy, equality, expanded reason, and a vigorous public sphere.

I argue in this book that the ideas of Dewey and Mills provide a philosophical and theoretical foundation for the development of a critical public sociology. I attempt to show that these men, taken together, offer the crucial elements of a holistic and grounded approach to social inquiry shaped by progressive values and a strong concern for a morally dedicated social science. In line with the genre of twentieth-century American social criticism but extending beyond it, the pragmatist thinking of Dewey and Mills was focused on problem solving and social change. Accordingly, both men regarded the social sciences as a means of promoting progress toward a better society.

The plan of this book is as follows. Beginning with a brief historical overview, Chapter 1 discusses the turn toward positivism and formalism and its dubious consequences for the field. Following a consideration of the problematic dualism of micro and macro analysis, the discussion turns to strategies for overcoming formalism by means of theoretical and methodological thinking oriented to the investigation of concrete, substantive problems.

After a presentation of the reformist views of Mills and Robert S. Lynd, Chapter 2 examines the tradition of social criticism inaugurated by Thorstein Veblen and inherited by the popular critics of post–World War II American society. This body of work is treated as illustrative of a type of sociological inquiry that is relevant, substantive, and public in nature. Aside from its contributions to the practice of social critique, the essential feature of this critical writing is the precedent it established for what I call "historical social psychology," a frame most evident in Mills's studies.

Chapter 3 turns to the philosophy of pragmatism, concentrating on the work of Dewey. Dewey's work is interpreted as providing a means of reorienting social science, social theory, and methodology away from formalist procedures toward a grounded mode of inquiry and analysis. Emphasis is placed on pragmatism's antiformalism and Dewey's antidualism. These epistemological positions are credited with providing a starting point for a substantive sociology based on the concrete, dynamic character of social life, captured in Dewey's concepts of experience and inquiry, as opposed to the abstract and static analytical categories of formalism.

Chapter 4 introduces a series of connections between Dewey and Mills, organized around the theme of the unity of theory and practice. This is discussed in terms of Dewey's conceptions of the relationship between thought and action, human life as problem solving, and the ubiquity and permanence of change. This framework is a basis for establishing continuities between Dewey and Mills and assessing the similarities and differences between them, especially regarding their views of social change and politics.

Finally, Chapter 5 begins with a critical discussion of the fact-value distinction and proceeds to an exploration of the normative character of social science employing the views of Hilary Putnam, Gunnar Myrdal, Max Weber, Mills, and Dewey. As a culmination of issues posed throughout the book, this chapter draws attention to the evaluative and critical features of Dewey's thought and pragmatism more generally, highlighting Dewey's advocacy of the moral and ethical character of science. All of these thinkers established ground for an objective conception of values that links sociological analysis to the tradition of critique. The notion of social critique is explored in relation to the neo-Marxist tradition of critical theory and to Dewey's pragmatism. The symbolic interactionist elements in Dewey's thought are put forth as offering the constituents of an expanded and more effective form of critique that improves on Frankfurt School theory while offering a concrete scientific and pluralistic approach to critique that is sociologically grounded.

1

Against Sociological Formalism

American sociology came into its own during the prosperous post–World War II period of expansion in higher education and social science research. This was a period marked by professionalization of the field and a preoccupation with scientific procedure involving the adoption of a positivist scientific outlook that took the natural sciences as a model for the practice of sociology. This period of rapid evolution in the discipline toward a new scientific agenda resulted in dramatic changes in the practice of sociology that featured a new formalism that put a premium on abstract theory and data analyses. These changes constituted a major shift in disciplinary priorities in which theory construction and methodological procedure took precedence over subject matter.

The new scientific orthodoxy eventually led to a reaction, precipitated by the social unrest and organized political movements of the 1960s and 1970s. Competing ideas, ideologies, theories, and research agendas came to challenge the positivist turn on grounds that it disconnected sociology from the realities of American life and emptied sociological ideas and concepts of their human content. Now a contested field, sociology entered a period of growing heterodoxy. While fragmenting the field, the array of new sociologies had one thing in common: opposition to the positivism and formalism accompanying the professionalization of the discipline during the 1940s and 1950s. This opposition was partially successful in bringing sociology down to earth, but the field has remained in relative disarray and largely divided between positivists and their antagonists ever since. As a consequence, despite encouraging trends toward renewal over the last fifty years, it can safely be said that sociology continues to seek a coherent identity and sense of relevance.

Sociology in the West was largely founded on nineteenth-century European social theory, a voluminous intellectual response to the social crises accompanying the rise of modernity. Classical social theory defined itself primarily through a body of ideas and observations about the nature of modernity and its impact on traditional social structures and patterns of thought. Emerging during a time of philosophical ferment and social and political upheavals, classical theory was fueled by a variety of intellectual currents and sociocultural outlooks. In seeking to identify the main contours of modernity, the early theorists focused their attention on processes of social change, specifically what they perceived as the dynamics and effects of industrialism, urbanization, expanding markets, bureaucracy, and democracy, along with new patterns of culture and ideology accompanying and driving these forces.[1]

With some exceptions, American sociologists today often fail to appreciate the contribution classical social theory made to the creation of the subject matter and major themes of the field. This body of theory was born of the massive sociocultural changes preceding and wrought by the rising market economy of industrial capitalism. The subject matter of sociology was thus initially forged from a cluster of historical, intellectual, and political concerns connected to this great transformation.

In the United States, sociology emerged in a substantially different set of conditions from those prevailing in Europe. Though the theoretical ideas of the Europeans offered some guidance, early American sociology was shaped by a philosophical and cultural orientation focused on the problems of a young, heterogeneous, and developing country. Early sociology in the United States was composed of a mix of classical European themes and a distinctively American engagement in empirical research. Unlike the European tradition, early American sociology was shaped by a set of moral concerns surrounding the social problems characterizing an ethnically diverse urban life and a nation in the process of painfully inventing itself. Given the differences between the New and Old Worlds, modernity in the United States was thus destined to acquire a more *practical* set of meanings than within European social theory.[2] At the same time, in the American context the pursuit of sociology was shaped less by intellectual concerns than by a moral ethos of social improvement.

This brief background can serve as a frame for examining the transition of the discipline of sociology at mid-twentieth century and its mixed consequences. Since that time, given the contrasts between the European tradition and the contested trajectory of American sociology, there has been a continuing conflict of opinions over the very meaning, purpose, and direction of the field. In what follows, a version of the issues at stake in the debate is briefly outlined in order to set the stage for a critique of the discipline.

The Rise of Positivism and Formalism

The University of Chicago is usually considered the birthplace of American sociology,[3] and the type of sociology incubated at this institution shaped the field for several decades.[4] While the European founders were a source of theoretical insights, the dominant influences at this institution were the homegrown pragmatist philosophies of John Dewey and George Herbert Mead.[5] These men were major figures at Chicago, and their ideas lent themselves to a socially engaged sociology in an era of business tycoons and rival progressive reformers. Tending to side with the latter, the social philosophy of pragmatism placed primary emphasis on democratic values, experimentation, and societal improvement through collective problem solving. These themes inspired many sociologists to engage in morally and politically concerned research into the problems of uprooted and marginal groups and immigrant ethnic communities struggling to survive amid the ills and predations of urban life. While not definitive of the entire field, this version of Chicago sociology established a strong precedent for the study of social problems while mirroring the politics of the Progressive Era.[6]

This variant of Chicago sociology had a strong presence in the discipline until the 1930s, when the social sciences began to enter a period of professionalization in their search for scientific identity and legitimacy (Haney 2008). During and following the crises of the Depression and European fascism, the field came under increasing pressure to prove its worth as a scientific discipline capable of addressing major societal problems, particularly the growing threats to democracy and social order posed by economic crisis, extremist ideologies, and widespread political conflict. These pressures undermined the earlier moral and practical concerns of sociologists, causing a major shift of orientation toward the cultivation of scientific technique. This soon led to a positivistic trend toward emulation of the natural sciences and the emergence of theory and research as the central concerns of the discipline.[7] While signaling a promising new phase of disciplinary progress, this transition meant a relative decline in substantive work and a new emphasis on scientific method. Perhaps most significant, this change of priorities entailed a distancing of sociology from its previous concern with social problems and its engagement in public life (Haney 2008, 9).

With this change of direction there appeared a new formalism, a mode of theoretical and methodological practice in which conceptual abstraction and scientific rigor take precedence over subject matter. For all practical purposes, formalism means that "form" trumps "content." But it also means that what goes on within the organized discipline, based on the specialized concepts and methods of trained sociologists, tends to overshadow events and developments in the world outside the university. With this shift, the natural science model of "detached" observation replaced the earlier, largely qualitative methods of the Chicago School, becoming the dominant investigative paradigm that shaped the field from the late 1940s through the early 1960s (Haney 2008, 9).[8]

These changes coincided with a transfer of the center of disciplinary gravity from Chicago to other universities, especially those on the East Coast. Under the sway of Talcott Parson's functionalist theory, Harvard became a center of abstract theorizing and system building. Simultaneously, through the work of Paul Lazarsfeld and his colleagues at the Bureau of Applied Social Research, Columbia University became known for its highly technical advances in data collection and quantitative analysis. Accompanying these developments was a growing sense that the pursuit of science and engagement with the public and its problems were incompatible goals. As sociology began to cloister itself in the academy and various research institutes, the dominant trend of the discipline was a turn away from social problems and the reformist orientation of the earlier generation (Haney 2008, 17). Reformism was now mostly displaced by a new professionalism dedicated to the pursuit of science on terms dictated primarily by well-resourced institutions connected to government and the new corporate economy.

A watershed moment, the rise of formalism manifested itself in two divides within the field. First, it created a tendency to separate conceptual issues from methodological technique and, correspondingly, theory from research. This split resulted in a growing gap between theoretical development and the accumulation of raw data. These changes were reflections of a profession now comprising specialists with increasingly narrow disciplinary interests, divided roughly between theorists and researchers. While leading scholars such as Talcott Parsons and Robert K. Merton urged a close connection between theory and empirical research,[9] in practice specialists in each area typically failed to link the two. Second, the turn to formalism resulted in a disjunction between two intellectual tendencies, styles, and disciplinary attitudes, namely, the "down-to-earth" orientation of those working in the tradition of Chicago and the abstract mode of functionalist theorizing and data analyses being pursued on the East Coast.

These changes were due less to the internal dynamics of the discipline, though these played an important part, than to external forces. The formalistic mode of inquiry that came with professionalization and "scientization,"[10] and the corresponding impoverishment of substantive work, was largely a response to national administrative and policy needs that arose during World War II, its aftermath, and the beginning of the Cold War. This was a period during which the disciplinary mainstream, seeking scientific legitimacy as a means of attracting resources, began to respond more directly to the specialized interests of government, big business, foundations, and other funding agencies, to the relative detriment of attention to problems of concern to the lay public.[11] The rush to align sociological practice with the methods and standards of the natural sciences was thus driven primarily by the growing demands of government and business and the need for greater material and institutional support for the discipline.[12] Eventually, as sociologists were called on to prove their worth as scientists, professionals, and academics, career and personal ambition emerged as prime motivations.

During this transition, the moral and political issues surrounding the earlier work on social problems were marginalized as enthusiasm grew for the ideals of "objectivity" and "scientific autonomy." Many of those identified with the Chicago tradition resisted this change of priorities, disavowing efforts to model sociology on the natural sciences and the withdrawal of the discipline into an ivory tower. This eventually created a rivalry between competing views of the role of sociology and its appropriate methodologies. The ensuing debates were initially focused less on the relationship of sociology to the moral and political concerns of sociologists who had worked in the Chicago tradition than on the theoretical and methodological issues posed by the positivist paradigm. These were not entirely separate concerns, and as these debates reached their zenith in the mid-to-late 1960s the larger societal and political context of sociology eventually emerged as a focal point of dissent for those seeking to develop a discipline of greater substance and relevance to the realities of American life.

The achievements of both the Chicago and the Harvard/Columbia traditions are worthy of our attention but are now largely a matter of history. The sociological landscape has changed dramatically since the 1960s, when social change forced a diversification of the discipline and growth in alternative perspectives and research agendas. But while functionalist forms of theorizing and the Parsonian mythology of consensus have largely vanished, a glance at the sociological literature suggests that a positivist model of inquiry persists in many areas of the discipline.[13] The split between theory and research and their subordination to the deterministic and mechanistic models and techniques of natural science have continued, however diminished their influence. This has meant a loss of balanced and comprehensive approaches to social life and social change in all their human and structural complexities.

The Dualism Problem

The relative isolation of sociology from the public and its problems is only one of the negative ramifications of formalism. Formalism has also contributed to the creation of artificial and misleading conceptual divisions that fragment our understanding of social structure and process. Perhaps the most obvious of these is the division between micro and macro perspectives and theories. The source of this division can be found in a subtle but highly consequential misstep. Formal theory has converted the real dual*ity* of social life—the difference between the actions of persons and the emergence of institutional and cultural structures—into an abstract dual*ism.* Once this happens, a series of dichotomies are substituted for a complex relationship of dynamic and evolving *tensions* between the two levels of associational life. Theoretical constructions that turn each level into a fixed category tend to empty the *interrelationship* between actor and society of any substantive content. The dualities in which these tensions inhere are thus treated as distinct entities rather than socially and historically situated dialectical relations between actors and structures.[14]

The intrusion of dualistic thinking into a field that formerly held to a more integrated and concrete view of society has had numerous adverse effects. "Actions" and "structures," "change" and "order," "meanings" and "facts" are terms that have been dichotomized and converted into abstractions that fail to represent empirical social reality. The staying power of these dualisms is an indication of the self-perpetuating nature of the formalist mode of analysis. Formalism feeds on abstraction, which invariably leads to the construction of dichotomous categories, which in turn perpetuate abstract modes of thought divorced from the interrelatedness and continuities of the real world.

The problem of dualism is certainly not exclusively the creation of formalistically minded sociologists. Dualistic thinking is not only embedded in our linguistic structure; it is also deeply rooted in Western thought. The individual-society distinction inheres in the subject-object opposition originating with the Greeks, developed in Kantian and Hegelian philosophy, and given rigid formulation as a fixed dichotomy by René Descartes. The rise of modern individualism reinforced this dualism by creating a *cultural* dichotomy of "individual *versus* society," suggesting a discordant relationship between thinking, willing, acting subjects and a world of external, impersonal forces seen as resistant or opposed to these subjects. Beginning in the nineteenth century, major strands of social theory have portrayed the social forces of modernity as beyond the control of individuals, as contravening human desire and intention (and the Enlightenment vision of rationality) by imposing limits on individuals' capacity to think and act freely and rationally. Generally speaking, modernist discourses have constructed the individual and society as opposing entities.[15] Both the epistemological dualism inherent in the structure of Western thought and the intellectual and cultural discourse of antagonism—which portrays a modernity divided against itself, celebrating the creative powers of the individual while simultaneously unleashing forces that thwart the individual—underwrite the gap sociological formalism has established between micro and macro phenomena.

Given this background, with the introduction of formalism the emergence of contending schools of thought partitioned by the micro-macro distinction would appear to have been inevitable. In keeping with its presumptive intellectual and scientific purposes, within this dualistic framework sociology has tended to subordinate the individual to society. This has taken two theoretical forms. On the one hand, society and culture have been simplistically theorized as constraining the individual.[16] On the other hand, these powerful entities have been theorized as both constraining and *enabling* the individual, a more nuanced conception developed in different ways by some of the classic European theorists and those in the American tradition, most notably George Herbert Mead.

Theoretical and philosophical issues notwithstanding, the rise of formalism is essentially a methodological problem. With formalism, variable, concrete connections between individuals and society acquire the status of static categories, creating a series of conceptual reifications.[17] "Actor" and "system," for example, become abstractions detached from social reality and substituted for real people and institutional structures. Arguably, the tendency toward conceptual reification is more likely to occur in more deterministically oriented theories and mechanical forms of causal explanations than in interpretively oriented approaches such as symbolic interactionism. The former, formalistic approaches are prone to the danger of "false realism," in which concepts tend to be treated as literal descriptions of reality. Formalistic theorizing thus contravenes the position of "nominalism," which treats concepts as mere *representations* of reality. It is no surprise that interpretive sociologists are more likely to be cautious of the error of treating ideas and concepts as real things rather than their representations. To repeat a well-worn but often forgotten axiom, the proper function of sociological concepts is heuristic and analytical, and they are not to be confused with actual phenomena.[18] Unlike interpretive theories, which are focused on "meaningful action/interaction," highly abstract, formal theoretical systems (for example, functionalism, systems theory, exchange theory) are most prone to the error of false realism. In general, the more positivistic variants of sociological theory tend to mistakenly treat concepts as actual objects.[19]

In sum, formalist dualisms create unnecessary problems. First, a formal separation of micro and macro forces us into a misleading epistemological choice: we can either (1) accept each level of analysis as a different way of looking at the same thing or (2) on the assumption that each provides only a partial perspective, we can attempt to connect or integrate them. While in certain situations both views could be defended, *only* the second option is acceptable as general methodological practice. Since emergent social phenomena are traceable to but not *reducible* to the actions of individuals, grounds exist for maintaining the macro-micro distinction as a heuristic device. The task of theorists and researchers, however, is to understand the *interrelatedness* of the different levels and to formulate empirically grounded propositions that *connect* them.[20]

For all practical purposes, formalism artificially divides the discipline into two sociologies (Dawe 1970). On the one hand, we have a sociology founded on positivist methods associated with the natural science model and largely macro in nature. On the other hand, there is a sociology of interpretation and meaning focused on the micro level of interaction, having strong affinities with what is often called the "human sciences."[21] And this has tended to be a lopsided division. Despite the significance of structural explanations, sociological positivism has often been guilty of a certain exaggeration of the effects of structure at the expense of action and agency. Thus, the interpretive school, mainly the symbolic interactionists, has rightly asserted that there has been a lack of attention in structural sociology to (1) notions of meaning, creativity, and innovation; (2) the connections of large-scale social phenomena to micro action and interaction processes; and (3) the cultural and social psychological sources of order and change, specifically how and to what extent variations in "system" states are a function of the definitional work and motivations of individuals.[22] The lesson to be drawn is that formulations that strike a balance between "determinist" and "nondeterminist" conceptions, social structure/culture and the individual, ought to be the practiced form of sociological description and explanation.

Toward a Substantive and Relevant Sociology

The theoretical and methodological perils of formalism are sufficient reason to reject this form of sociological practice. But formalism has larger ramifications. Under its influence, mainstream sociology by and large continues to labor under a disciplinary regime too ingrown and overspecialized to provide a truly substantive, comprehensive, and integrated picture of society, one that captures the lived realities of society and group life. The discipline's preoccupation with scientific procedure and its corresponding remoteness from public life has its counterpart in the relative absence of an intellectual/scientific agenda that would engage serious moral, ethical, and political questions about the state of society and the problems of its members.[23]

All sciences depend on a logically organized body of concepts, principles, and procedures that can serve as a framework for generating and testing hypotheses. Sociological formalism, however, is formal sociology that has acquired a life of its own. To work in a formalistic mode is to evade the task of constructing sociological explanations and understandings that are faithful to reality and that offer concrete and accessible knowledge to nonsociologists.[24]

Once theory and research succumb to a preoccupation with technique, these become ends in themselves, and sociology is reduced to a barren exercise in scientific procedure, such as modeling statistical relationships. Excessive abstraction contributes to a bifurcation of the field into theoretical analysis and data collection, to the detriment of both. This double tendency was the target of the well-known statement of C. Wright Mills in *The Sociological Imagination,* in which he attacked postwar American sociology for its turn to "grand theory" and "abstracted empiricism" (Mills 1961, chaps. 2 and 3). In both cases, as Mills rightly saw, sociologists were indulging in abstract constructions at the expense of real empirical content.

As suggested by Mills's critique, excessive abstraction, characteristic of systems theory but not uncommon in garden-variety sociology, has been perhaps the most intractable problem. Appealing to "classic social analysis," implying mainly the European theorists, Mills advocated instead a sociology concerned with "historical social structures" (Mills 1961, 21). Here, he is suggesting that to avoid unnecessary abstraction that fails to reflect the reality of social phenomena, sociological analysis, while concerned with the individual, needs always to remain focused on the structural, historical, and cultural dimensions of society, or what he thought of as "the big picture" (Aronowitz 2012, chap. 8; Mills 1961, 17).

To the extent that sociology began to show some aversion to positivism and change direction in the 1960s, much of this change can indeed be credited to the work of Mills, for many the icon of critical sociology. For Mills, truly meaningful social analysis is contextualized in the situated problems of human actors, problems that in turn were to be connected to the large-scale forces shaping them. With insight into what went wrong with the discipline, he gave us a vision and model of a nonformalist sociology of substance, human significance, and social, moral, and political relevance (Mills 1961). He saw this as a matter of turning "personal problems" into "public issues" (ibid., chap. 1). For Mills, sociology's mission was to examine how societies affect the people who live in them and by implication to suggest how people, whether in possession of power or subject to it, might think and act in ways that would alter the condition of their lives. In parallel fashion, Mills called on sociology to examine the relationship between biography and history. He understood that forgetting the historically specific nature of social facts is to premise sociology on the mistaken belief that its object of study is a static entity exhibiting characteristics of a universal, unchanging nature. In reality, society is a historical entity, a changeful system of dynamic forces and relations composed of social structures and an ensemble of active agents. What Mills in effect proposed in his statements about biography and history was that the formal division of micro and macro be *translated back* into concrete human terms, thereby connecting the two levels in formulations reflecting actual social and historical relationships.[25]

Many in the field have averted the formalistic straitjacket by pursuing a variety of original and socially grounded work that reflects Mills's call for sociological substance. While acknowledging these trends, following Mills I would propose two key principles on which to develop a more relevant and substantive sociology. First, to avoid unnecessary abstraction, it is imperative that sociologists devote themselves to the study of *particular substantive areas* as opposed to the development of theoretical structures and methodological technique. Second, a steadfast concern for the *source* of the *chronic problems* plaguing society and its individual members would keep sociological inquiry focused on the concrete realities of actors and social structures and the interrelated institutional workings of the system as a whole.[26] A major goal of this type of inquiry would be to develop workable, scientifically based remedies for lessening or abolishing the harmful social and human effects of poorly functioning institutions. In this respect, sociological inquiry needs to move beyond conventional definitions of social problems to include the entire panoply of ailments afflicting highly bureaucratized, market-based societies, of which the United States is the prime example. This would require sociologists to more openly and honestly acknowledge the nature of the society in which Americans live and to focus attention on its problematic characteristics.

Such a sociology, to my mind, would attempt to represent and analyze the following features of contemporary American life. Fueled by the profit motive, economic modernity has created an essentially acquisitive society,[27] whose dominant behavior patterns are at best uncaring of others and at worst predatory. As the textbook case of this societal type, American society is driven by an ethos of self-reliance that celebrates competitive individualism and private gain. These are cultural and psychological traits indispensable to the profit-oriented agenda of consumer capitalism and an economy dependent on a "free" market in exploited labor. Chronic problems of alienation, feelings of powerlessness, social inequality, violence, the corrupting power of money, ego and celebrity worship, and the consequent erosion of democracy—all are familiar features of life under a system that routinely favors private advantage over public good. Situating social problems in the context of these features of capitalism, a historically specific type of society, would be a necessary step toward the creation of a more relevant and socially or humanly useful sociology.

A considerable amount of contemporary sociological work already approximates a socially concerned and critical social science engaged in exposing and accounting for these problems. The piecemeal approach of much of this work, however, falls short of providing a comprehensive picture of these problems' *systemic origins*. The discipline sorely lacks analyses of large-scale historical, cultural, and social processes, analyses without which social problems cannot be adequately explained, understood, and mitigated. This would entail abandoning an abstract, generalizing sociology in favor of one that studies society in terms of its particular historical and cultural formations and configurations. This sociology would be less universalistic and more provincial and at the same time less piecemeal and more comprehensive.[28]

Without underestimating the value of much contemporary work or harboring illusions about the likelihood of dramatic disciplinary change in the near future, I explore in Chapter 2 an earlier tradition of sociological inquiry that exemplifies what might be thought of as "sociology-on-the-ground" or "sociology-with-human-significance." This is a sociology that addresses real problems with breadth and insight, without unnecessary abstraction and jargon, one that provides an understanding of our lives through thoughtful and unsentimental criticism of existing sociocultural arrangements and priorities. Perhaps most important, this is a sociology that encourages self-reflection and self-understanding. It does so by means of a sociological critique that assertively questions how we currently organize our lives, individually and collectively, and in terms that nonspecialists can grasp and, I hope, act on.

2

C. Wright Mills and the Tradition of Social Criticism

The "promise" of sociology that C. Wright Mills describes in the opening of *The Sociological Imagination* (1961, chap. 1) can be thought of in a variety of ways. What most immediately comes to mind, however, is the scope and diversity of the field and the power of sociological explanation. While its breadth of subject matter might seem a liability, the reach and versatility of sociology offers, as Mills rightly saw, the possibility of a comprehensive picture of society and the lives of its members.

Mills's own work exemplifies the creative potentials of the sociological perspective, demonstrating how it can illuminate the relationship between individual and society, actor and structure, social life and history. Mills believed that sociology ought to be used to further our understanding of social life and human beings as products of "historical social structures" (1961, 21). Focusing on "character" and "social structure" (Gerth and Mills 1964), Mills throughout much of his writing sought to portray individuals in terms of the historically specific social and cultural patterns within which they lived and acted. For Mills, sociology's "promise" resided in what he called "the sociological imagination . . . which enables us to grasp history and biography and the relations between the two within society" (1961, 6).

Mills made good use of sociology's porous boundaries and the field's capacity for empirical discovery. He astutely navigated the social sciences' common borders, believing that disciplinary specialization was largely an artifice of professionalization that fragmented our knowledge and understanding. Indeed, Mills was in a sense ahead of his time in cultivating the practice of "interdisciplinary" work, although this term certainly does not describe his approach. As he saw the matter, the excesses of formalization, generalization, and abstraction—and the tendency to separate theory from method, specializing in one or the other—could be counteracted only by engaging in "empirical studies of contemporary social facts and problems" (1961, 23). If there is to be specialization, it should proceed not along disciplinary lines but in terms of "problem-areas." Attempts to "integrate the social sciences" should be done not in terms of "conceptions and methods" but in terms of "problems and subject matters" (41). By Mills's own example, this meant stepping outside of conventional disciplinary boundaries to draw on any material relevant to a particular problem. Indeed, as Mills argues, this is hardly different from the practices of the classic theorists themselves, including Émile Durkheim, who is often credited with establishing sociology as a scientific discipline.[1] Finally, if there is any confusion regarding what happens to the role of the sociologist when all the social sciences are in play, Mills says, "What is specifically 'sociological' in the study of any particular feature of a total society is the continual effort to relate that feature to others, in order to gain a conception of the whole" (137). The province of sociology is thus the whole social structure or system.

Given its broad perspective, and its relevance to the public, sociology's relationship to journalism is no less important, as Mills demonstrated by the style and tone of his writing. Strictly speaking not a social science, journalism has always shared a close but uneasy relationship with sociology, with skeptics in the latter field often looking down on journalism for its alleged lack of theory and scientific rigor. Nonetheless, despite its reputation as a "soft" or "quasi" social science, in subject matter and even method journalism and sociology frequently overlap. As a form of reporting on matters of public interest, journalism has obvious ramifications for the kind of sociology advocated by Mills. Sociologically informed studies employing journalistic methods and reporting styles can provide rich portrayals of human behavior and ways of life along with information presented in a form accessible to nonacademic readers. As for impact on the public, many of the most influential books on politics and public policy have been written by journalists, some of whom possess research skills of the highest quality.

Both questions—sociology's relationship to the other social sciences and to journalism—were an essential aspect of Mills's critique of professional sociology. As questions having a direct bearing on the central theme of Chapter 1—formalism, positivism, and professionalism as barriers to a publicly relevant sociology grounded in everyday life—these were questions of direct pertinence to Mills. Gatekeepers still frequently regard appropriation of material from nonsociologists a dubious practice, despite lack of compelling evidence that either an interdisciplinary or journalistic approach involves a compromise in scientific standards. In any event, before a fuller discussion of Mills and the genre of publicly oriented social criticism to which he contributed, we need to consider further means of combatting formalistic sociology.

Overcoming Formalism: Grounding Strategies

In addition to interdisciplinary and journalistic connections, there are approaches internal to the discipline offering useful ideas for situating sociological analysis in lived realities. The well-known Grounded Theory of Barney Glaser and Anselm Strauss (2010), for instance, offers a *methodological* protocol for generating theory inductively from data rather than deductively from formal concepts and axioms. While it is intended for use by qualitative researchers, the authors claim that Grounded Theory is applicable in *any* sociological study. Indeed, the authors' position is that "there is no fundamental clash between the purposes and capacities of qualitative and quantitative methods or data" (ibid., 17).

What Glaser and Strauss propose is a program for practicing sociology with a methodology aimed at the collection of raw data. While

Grounded Theory is a remedy for many of the deficiencies of formalism, however, it is lacking in theoretical content. What Glaser and Strauss underplay is the role that theory plays in organizing social phenomena into conceptually distinct and significant objects of investigation. In short, theory assigns *meaning* to data. While the authors claim their research approach strengthens theory, it actually segregates the research process. Despite its virtues, by leaning on method Grounded Theory tends to preoccupy itself with procedure at the expense of substantive theorizing.

Grounding sociological inquiry is often less a matter of research methodology than of *subject matter* and *theoretical structure.* Mills understood that theory is the means by which social phenomena are defined, framed, treated, and presented, but he goes a step further, asserting that social research and its findings require a theoretical apparatus that draws on social structure and history (1961, chaps. 1 and 4). In his view, the "facts" of milieux—the small-scale (ibid., 78) social and institutional settings in which people live, work, and act—are to be grasped in terms of larger social and historical entities.

Mills's injunction to focus sociological attention on "problems" rather than theory and method raises the question of what constitutes a "problem." For Mills, problems were essentially "human problems." In turn, he believed that genuine insight into the nature and source of human problems would require sociologists to conceptualize society in terms of historically specific social structures. Problems, Mills thought, were to be explained with reference to the connections between the troubles of individuals and the institutional and systemic forces shaping their lives. And Mills always made clear that such explanations would involve analyzing structures of inequality and power, a central theme in his work. This implies conducting social inquiry with a strong eye for the economic and political factors conditioning social life.

In recent decades there has been an encouraging trend toward these kinds of inquiry. At the same time, the unfortunate practice of assigning the study of inequality and power to subfields of the discipline (e.g., stratification, political sociology) ignores the fact that inequality and power are features of *all* social relations. Demoting these topics to the status of subfields minimizes their analytical importance and their connection to personal and social problems. Though interested in the subjective dimensions of behavior, Mills believed material interests and power relations were often just as important as culture and ideology in explaining social process and the psychology of individuals.

The social problems studies of the early American sociologists offer some precedent for this type of work. The Chicago School research into the urban landscape of crime, poverty, and race/ethnic relations displayed a strong empirical orientation to the concrete problems of people's lives. Nonetheless, these studies were for the most part weak on issues of inequality and power, and by focusing on community problems, examples of Mills's "milieux," this work lacked adequate theoretical scope for linking social problems to large-scale historical and structural change. This established within the discipline a piecemeal pattern of social inquiry marked by a tendency to separate the parts from the whole, the main object of Mills's critique of the discipline.

As against Grounded Theory and the Chicago School, Mills felt that classical European theory continued to provide the backbone of sociological inquiry.[2] In their analyses of the sweeping historical changes shaping modern society, thinkers like Durkheim and Simmel and particularly Marx and Weber remain models of theoretical grounding. These thinkers closely examined the characteristic features and impact of modern capitalism. In an era prior to the rise of the specialized social sciences, Marx and Weber drew on a variety of scholarly resources—especially history—in theorizing connections between social actors and the structural and ideational elements of society. Despite Weber's greater appreciation of the complexity of cultural factors in the formation of belief systems and patterns of action, both thinkers enriched their ideas by contextualizing sociological phenomena in history and social change.[3]

While many sociologists have continued to draw on the work of the classics, if alive today Mills would probably regard the bulk of American sociology as only peripherally related to the classic tradition because of its frequent failure to connect milieux to social structure and history. Mills's oeuvre, and specifically his arguments for linking biography and history, personal troubles and public issues, while displaying a characteristically American concern for the individual, aimed to reverse this tendency by developing an expansive "macro" perspective. With themes and insights drawn from the classics, particularly Weber, Mills attempted to synthesize a range of ideas he saw as relevant for explaining contemporary problems of milieux in terms of larger structural and cultural trends. Mills's accomplishments in this respect remain a model for a sociology that concretely combines micro and macro perspectives.

Looking back to Mills, finally, puts us in touch with a tradition just as important as that of the early Chicago generation and the classic European theorists. Mills was a key figure in the social criticism literature that flowered after World War II, involving numerous best-selling authors who popularized the social sciences with their provocative criticisms of postwar society. Before considering this work, however, I examine an allied body of criticism. Mills was an outspoken critic of American social science, building on the earlier critical reflections of Robert S. Lynd, who famously attacked social science for failing its responsibility to produce comprehensive and socially useful knowledge.

Reforming Social Science: Robert S. Lynd and C. Wright Mills

The emerging scientific priorities of the late 1930s, which pushed social science in a positivist and professionalizing direction, contributed to the formation of specialized disciplines with relatively distinct agendas and areas of inquiry. Responding to this trend, a few thoughtful scholars began to question the rationale of the social sciences and their place in society. Of special concern were questions about the social responsibility of these disciplines, specifically what purposes they were to serve and for whom.

The earliest and boldest statement came in 1939 from the Columbia University sociologist Robert S. Lynd in his book *Knowledge for What?* (1939). Lynd's critique, projecting a sense of urgency during the Great Depression and the rise of fascism in Europe, continues to resonate a sense of pressing need in our own era of ongoing crises. The striking sense of familiarity evoked by his remarks on the influence of businessmen and university bureaucrats on the social sciences and the latter's complicity with the status quo serves to illustrate the currency of Lynd's worries. While the context of Lynd's critique was the massive economic, social, and political failures of the 1930s, his view of the situation of the social sciences was prescient of postwar developments in academia.

Lynd begins by arguing that the social sciences are part of the wider culture and therefore bear an obligation to bring the knowledge they produce into the public arena in a manner that benefits the interests of society. On the question of how the social sciences were to fulfill this obligation, he presents a twofold critique. First, their proper focus should be the "whole culture," and this means pulling together findings from the various fields to create an overall picture of society as it actually exists in the lives of its members. Lynd places the burden of this task squarely on sociology. In Lynd's judgment, this was the one social science claiming to study "the whole," while in practice the sociological specialist had tended to "abstract his problem from its context" (1939, 21), leading to an "atomized" sociology lacking a comprehensive picture. In his words:

> The failure of the social sciences to think through and to integrate their several responsibilities for the common problem of relating their analysis of the parts to the analysis of the whole constitutes one of the major lags crippling their utility as human tools of knowledge. (Ibid., 15)

To correct this failing, the social sciences needed to adopt an inclusive "frame of reference," which would be the totality of culture in which all of the problems they studied could be situated. Lynd thus proposes the concept of culture as the unifying framework of a social science capable of an understanding based on the way people actually live.[4]

Second, Lynd argues at length for the analytical importance of "the individual," in his view the main constituent of culture, and for the need to retrieve the human element from behind the conceptual abstractions of the social sciences. He laments the "unfortunate dualism" between the individual and culture that emerges once the latter comes to be regarded as a "self-contained universe" existing apart from the person. Under these conditions, social science creates "another reified entity" that separates social analysis from how people actually think, feel, and behave. To counteract this tendency, he proposes reinstating the person as an analytical equal to culture and institutions. He also takes social scientists to task for forgetting that "useful conceptual discriminations are true only to a certain extent, as methodological tools." As to the problem of reified conceptual abstractions, Lynd is quite direct.

> The emphasis upon persons as the active carriers, perpetrators, and movers of culture performs for us the indispensable service of resolving the dualism of "culture *and* person," and of placing the primary emphasis where it basically belongs, upon people. (Italics in original)

For Lynd, the analyst must at some point move to the level of individual behavior; research that remains at the "institutional level" can give us only "crude and limited understandings" (1939, 21–25).

We can hardly miss the resemblances between Lynd's prewar critique and the later appraisal by C. Wright Mills in *The Sociological Imagination* (1961). Appearing toward the end of a singular career in sociology, Mills's book is in many respects an impassioned summing up of his scholarly endeavors and concerns. Written as both a critique of the discipline and a handbook for practicing sociologists, Mills's text draws attention to how inquiry focused on the relationship between biography and history infuses sociological work with human significance. Mills's emphasis on biography is an elaboration of Lynd's earlier plea to reinstate the individual person in social scientific analysis. The two men seem in full agreement that the social sciences should assume responsibility for producing knowledge that is of benefit to both individuals and society-at-large, with an analytical understanding of the interrelationship between the two. Finally, both scholars courageously address the question of values, arguing that social science acquires genuine cultural and human meaning only to the extent that the problem of values is made explicit in both its subject matter and the practices of social scientists themselves.

Yet, as the title suggests, *The Sociological Imagination* goes beyond Lynd's critique of the narrow disciplinary restrictions of the social sciences. Mills moves closer to a vision of a sociology of human relevance and substance that connects culture and social structure to persons. In the main body of the book Mills offers an overview of the character and makeup of American society and its historical situation, setting forth guidelines for how sociologists might realize his conception of the sociological enterprise. Exhibiting a range of knowledge and a full grasp of pertinent philosophical issues, Mills lucidly discusses the broad intellectual and social contexts of the field. He points especially to the pressing questions these larger contexts pose for sociologists who would seek understanding of the impact on the individual of a modernizing, depersonalized, bureaucratized world.

The heart of his critique is contained in the first chapter, "The Promise." In lively and engaging prose, Mills makes an appeal for studying society from the standpoint of its *human* problems. First of all, to formulate the connection between "the personal troubles of milieu and the public issues of social structure" it is necessary to "ask what values are cherished yet threatened, and what values are cherished and supported, by the characterizing trends of our period" (Mills 1961, 6, 11). Against the grain of the discipline, Mills places the question of values squarely at the center of sociological inquiry. Underscoring the importance of values, he voices worry of widespread unawareness or unconcern among the public that cherished values are indeed at risk. Mills refers to a collective sense of "indifference," leading to "apathy," and "uneasiness" or "anxiety" over the importance of values in people's lives.

Second, while perhaps wishfully projecting his own hopes onto others, there is a compelling quality to the claim Mills makes about individuals' desire for knowledge of themselves and the everyday world they inhabit. Questioning the adequacy of contemporary mass fiction for a sufficient understanding of modern problems, Mills states, "It is social and historical reality that men want to know. . . . They yearn for facts, they search for their meanings, they want a 'big picture' in which they can believe and within which they can come to understand themselves" (1961, 17). Here Mills claims to perceive a dire public need for a body of social knowledge that would help ordinary people comprehend the reality of their complex and confusing lives. In this respect, he is pointing to a supposed void that only a sociology linking personal life to larger social structures could fill.

Third, in a minor reversal of Lynd's complaint about lack of attention to the person, Mills demurs at the postwar turn to individual psychology that tends to reduce personal troubles to "human nature" while ignoring the strong influence of social structure. Attacking the claim of the prominent Freudian scholar Ernest Jones that the person's "chief enemy and danger is his own unruly nature and the dark forces pent up within him," Mills argues:

> On the contrary: "Man's chief danger" lies in the unruly forces of contemporary society itself, with its alienating methods of production, its enveloping techniques of political domination, its international anarchy—its pervasive transformations in the very "nature" of man and the conditions and aims of his life. (1961, 3)

As a passionate expression of Mills's conviction that the source of human troubles is an inhumane society that regards people as grist for its economic and political mill, this statement is vaguely laden with Marxist themes. Mills thus takes a strong stand against the privatization of individuals' problems and their relegation to the realm of private therapy, pointing a finger at a society that fails the individual and is thus in need of extensive *sociological* diagnosis.[5]

Finally, in his opening chapter Mills refers to his own biases as a sociologist and social thinker, calling on other social scientists to make their biases explicit. This is Mills at his best as a forthright and candid scholar of intellectual integrity, suggesting that it is incumbent on all social scientists to be self-reflexive in their work. Mills's call for reflexivity is yet another appeal to put values at the forefront of sociological inquiry and to treat them as not only intrinsic to social life but crucial to the thinking and practices of sociologists. In his words, disclosing one's biases leads to "greater self-awareness all around—which is of course a precondition for objectivity in the enterprise of social science as a whole" (1961, 21).

Mills concludes this discussion by invoking what he calls "classic social analysis." Though failing to explain exactly what he means by this term, he alludes to classic European social theory and its derivatives when he says, "Its essential feature is the concern with *historical social structures;* and that its problems are of direct relevance to urgent public issues and insistent human troubles" (1961, 21; italics added). Mills sees "great obstacles" to the continuation of this tradition, but he also believes that "the qualities of mind that constitute it are becoming a common denominator of our general cultural life . . . and are coming to be felt as a need" (ibid.). This comment, too, begs crucial questions and perhaps sounds overly optimistic. But it reveals Mills's belief that, in spite of historical trends that he laments—bureaucratization, a concentration of power, the growth of mass culture—there is evidence of an enlarged intellectual awareness in the general population.[6]

Conscientious and articulate intellectuals of their times, Lynd and Mills remain unsurpassed as critics of modern social science. Each wrote within a different historical context, but their adverse reactions to the state of sociology converged in a set of common themes. Their prescriptions for change reflect different intellectual and ideological dispositions, with Lynd stressing the need for a unification of social science findings and Mills proposing a renewal of classical social theory's historical perspective on the character and consequences of a rapidly emerging modern society. Finally, in the face of ascendant positivism, both men showed uncommon courage in the attention they gave to values and in their call to reorient sociology away from scientific technique toward an engagement with human problems.

The Postwar Social Critics: Historical/Structural Social Psychology

In the work of Mills, sociology faced a provocative challenge to its sense of mission and purpose. This challenge was the achievement of a bold and ecumenical thinker whose relatively short life and career were marked by several shifts in theoretical orientation and research interests. Indeed, despite the clarity and outspokenness of his work, the changing trajectory and intricate structure of Mills's sociology became sources of a disputed reputation. Working within the tensions of numerous intellectual and political tendencies, Mills conveyed an ambiguous public persona, giving rise to varied and sometimes mistaken interpretations of the man and his goals. Despite his popular image as a political renegade and academic outsider, Mills was very much an academic person throughout his entire career, striving to transform sociology from within while attempting to engage a nonacademic reading public from without.[7]

Schooled in philosophy and early on an initiate of pragmatism, Mills was dedicated to the idea of a rigorous but humanly meaningful social science that grasped the larger structural and historical contexts of contemporary life. At the same time, Mills wanted a sociology critically engaged with the lives of real people and committed to the amelioration of social problems and the troubles of individuals. Even as he turned to classic European social theory, not unlike Lynd there was in Mills an ingrained American concern for the individual. Mills accordingly devoted himself to the task of delineating the social forces affecting ordinary lives.

Although Mills had a unique presence in the postwar intellectual scene, he was in the company of a number of popular and influential critics of midcentury America who shared many of his ideals and worries and who also worked within a perspective of historical and social change. While an heir of Lynd's critique of social science, Mills is thus equally important as a figure in a lineage of critical social theory and commentary that began with the founder of American social criticism, Thorstein Veblen (1934).[8] While Veblen's powerful insights and uniquely provocative and witty style of criticism remain unmatched, his influence has been widespread, mainly in the form of a mode of inquiry that coalesced among a number of social critics following World War II.

There is both irony and poetic justice in the fact that this group of writers emerged during the professionalization of academic sociology associated with the rise of positivist methods and formalistic approaches. Indeed, their writings were in large measure a *response* to these scientistic trends and served as their counterpoint.[9] These critics wrote animated and sometimes biting criticisms of American society in the 1950s and 1960s, conducting a type of critical social inquiry implicitly endorsed by Lynd and Mills in their critiques of sociology and manifested in Mills's own studies.

In retrospect, one is struck by the sense of history and the astute sociological insights of these writers. Consistent with Mills's emphasis on historical perspective, these critics approached society as a sociocultural configuration comprehensible only in historical context. In doing so, these authors cultivated a distinctive nondenominational form of critical writing, ignoring the boundaries of professional academic disciplines.

Perhaps most important was these critics' focus on the subjective and psychological dimensions of change. Given their framing of social problems, the ultimate concern of these writers was the fate of "Man" in modern capitalist society.[10] While not always cast in this language, for all practical purposes these writings were about the social and human consequences of a bureaucratized and corporatizing form of consumer capitalism. Their focus was the effects of structural and cultural change on the person-on-the-street, whom these critics saw as bereft of a sense of place and meaning in a world increasingly impersonal and uncertain. If these thinkers were following Mills's dictum of connecting history and biography, for them it meant illuminating the impact of a modernizing and affluent way of life on the consciousness and behavior of human actors.[11]

The defining feature of this writing was a sustained interest in the emerging personality and character structures of postwar America.[12] Mills was a leading figure in this movement. While engaged in a number of his own empirical research projects, he spent a number of years coauthoring a book with his teacher and colleague Hans Gerth, titled *Character and Social Structure* (1964) and subtitled "The Psychology of Social Institutions." In this underappreciated work, the authors present a comprehensive theoretical overview of the relationship between social and character structure, employing historical and comparative methods. Intended as a formal statement of the social structural sources of human behavior, this study demonstrates Mills's interest in a methodology for analyzing the institutional bases of character formation. In keeping with a fashion of the times,[13] the book was a study in social psychology, but one that outlined Mills's own methodological program for connecting biography to history and private troubles to public issues. In the preface, the authors offer a succinct statement of how they conceived of this area of study.

> The structural and historical features of modern society must be connected with the most intimate features of man's self. That is what social psychology is all about. (Gerth and Mills 1964, xix)

This statement represents a decisive departure from common definitions of social psychology, then and now, and serves as a summing up of the general approach of the social critics of the time, all of whom can be characterized as practicing a social psychology based on structural and historical analysis.

The best-known example of this approach is unquestionably David Riesman's 1950 publication, *The Lonely Crowd,* written with Nathan Glazer and Reuel Denny (Riesman, Glazer, and Denny 1961). Riesman discusses the role of changing demographics, increased social mobility, and economic change in the transition from a production to a consumption society, a process he sees as bringing about a transformation in personality types. The "traditional" personality of preindustrial culture gave way, during the rise of industrial production, to a transitional, "inner-directed" type of personality based on the internalization of parental authority. This type was followed in the contemporary period, with the rise of consumption relations, by the "other-directed" personality, a type of person dependent on the behavioral cues of others. In Riesman's view, the individual living under modern social structures develops a kind of "radar" that attunes behavior situationally to the pressures of peer group, school, and the mass media, socializing agencies and reference groups largely replacing the influences of family, religion, and neighborhood. In short, for Riesman contemporary social life called on individuals to adapt their attitudes and behavior to the expectations of a wide circle of "others," leading to a posture of conformity. A classic study, *The Lonely Crowd* exemplifies the kind of inquiry that tells us about the character type called forth by a given social structure and cultural/ideological pattern.

Another highly influential book on character type was *The Organization Man* by William H. Whyte (1956). Paralleling Riesman's argument, Whyte maintained that the individualistically oriented Protestant Ethic had in the age of large corporations given way to a new Social Ethic, shifting the person's orientation from one's inner beliefs toward a sense of obligatory adjustment to the organization. In Whyte's view, a sacrifice of inner convictions and individual initiative and creativity had become a social imperative. More importantly, it had become the basis of a new type of individual overly responsive to group pressures and adhering to an ideology of "belongingness."

Representing a distinctive approach to social analysis, Mills, Riesman, Whyte, and other critics of the time were engaged in what might be called "historical/structural social psychology." An admittedly unwieldy term, this label aptly describes the kind of inquiry begun by Veblen, continued by the postwar critics, formalized by Gerth and Mills, and practiced by Mills. Avoiding formal divisions between "micro" and "macro," this mode of analysis attempted to weave together a picture of the person who typified the American population (white, middle class, male) during the postwar period. These writers variously portrayed a character structure linked to the ascendancy of a social system driven by monetary rewards, increasing affluence, the pursuit of technology, and rapid growth in bureaucratic organization. Attuned to the ways that social structures and institutions formed characterological and behavioral traits, these critics saw the social psychology of everyday American life as an outgrowth of market-based social relations and a pecuniary culture. They perceived the rise of a prosperous middle class, whose lifestyle was consumerism, suburbia, and white-collar work, in terms of new values and ideologies endorsing a drive for social success through status competition and social conformity.

For most of these writers the growing influence of corporations, government, and other large organizations meant a loss of individuality and personal autonomy as well as a troubling concentration of organizational power. These critics examined how new structural and cultural forces were (mis)shaping who and what we were: our sense of self, our behavioral and dispositional traits, our inner experience, our emotional lives, and our ties or lack thereof to others. Avoiding formal analytical categories and the artificial gap these created between person and institutional/structural influences, these critics employed a historically based, structurally and culturally oriented conception of the person that concretized connections between the two levels.

In the attention they gave to the sources of character type these thinkers set forth a number of important sociological themes. Reading these authors with these themes in mind imparts a sense of unity to their work and draws attention to some enduring issues for practicing sociologists today.

The most obvious theme, beginning with Veblen and recurring throughout the criticism of the 1950s and 1960s, was the impact of material abundance. In *The Theory of the Leisure Class* (1934), first published in 1899, the commanding material prosperity of the upper classes in late-nineteenth-century America was seen by Veblen as turning the possession and display of material goods into invidious expressions of wealth and high status. In his account of the rise of "conspicuous consumption" in a society marked by pecuniary emulation, Veblen highlighted the consequences of consumer goods for the social norms governing class structure. Rising abundance made possible the transformation of the material possessions of the rich into legitimate and highly prized symbols of pecuniary success and a life of leisure. More important than his mere description of leisure-class behavior, however, was Veblen's argument that the power of these success symbols gave rise to emulative character traits in the *whole society*, generating a dynamic of status emulation extending throughout the entire class system.[14]

The theme of abundance becomes even more explicit in postwar assessments of the social and psychological effects of spreading prosperity. In his collection of wide-ranging essays of the late 1940s, titled *Abundance for What?* (1993), David Riesman thematizes material abundance in discussing a vast array of topics in the spheres of leisure, politics, and education. In *The Waste Makers* (1960), Vance Packard draws readers' attention to the wastefulness (for Veblen the hallmark of conspicuous consumption) of endless spending on material goods and the behavioral traits resulting from this trend. In *The Hidden Persuaders* (1957), the rise of a vast advertising industry exploiting the visual powers of television and the design and fashion industries enabled Packard to go much further than Veblen by exposing the new levers of motivational control over consumer behavior. This book was a provocative exposé of the methods used in what Paul A. Baran and Paul M. Sweezy in *Monopoly Capital* (1968) called "the sales effort." Picking up the main thread of Veblen's argument, Packard in *The Status Seekers* (1959) documents the many ways in which goods possession and social behavior mark a person's class status. A final example is a work more historically and technically oriented than Packard's trilogy: *The Affluent Society* (1958), by the prominent economist John Kenneth Galbraith, situates American prosperity economically rather than socially and culturally. Galbraith makes his most significant argument in one of his shortest chapters, "The Dependence Effect." Against the orthodoxy of the time, Galbraith claims that a dynamic of consumer manipulation is *inherent* in the economic system of capitalism: goods production itself is the source of consumer need/want. Whereas in the "conventional wisdom" (ibid., chap. 2) production is a response to consumer demand, in Galbraith's argument consumer demand is a function of productive output, since the latter sets the living standard at any given point in time. Along with the sales effort, production itself plays a crucial role in the status game, since the number and kind of goods in the marketplace effectively shape the field, thus determining the material contours and parameters of the game.[15]

As the central framework for examining changing social character, material abundance (most of the time and for an increasing number of people) beginning in the late 1940s changed society and its middle-class members in fundamental ways. Accordingly, the phenomenal growth of mass consumption and consumerism was the wellspring of numerous critical essays on American life. As the critics demonstrated, these developments had major implications for sociological analysis. For instance, in a number of works there appeared a politically controversial suggestion that a relative decline in the importance of economic production meant that problems of material inequality and insecurity had been superseded by a set of psychological problems related to the dynamics of a mass-consumption society, in which status concerns became paramount. Although more recent scholars have tended to frame consumption as a *cultural* phenomenon, the 1950s critics drew attention to how social organization and practices, in both work and leisure, had been fundamentally altered by the new consumer economy. While it is now commonplace to think of institutions such as the family, schools, hospitals, business enterprises, government agencies, the mass media, and more recently the Internet, as increasingly molded by the imperatives of a consumption economy, study of this basic aspect of contemporary social change has been mostly missing from the agendas of sociologists. In reality, processes of commodification and marketization have played a central role in shaping social relations and individual attitudes and dispositions. Implicitly drawing on the Weberian perspective of bureaucracy and the theory of the commodity form advanced by Marxist theory, these critics addressed a corpus of problems using theoretical tools still relevant today for understanding the essential features of American life.

The critical writings of this period paid relatively little attention to changes in the social class structure, with two important exceptions. Whyte's *The Organization Man* and Mills's *White Collar* addressed the rise of a new middle class that they saw as bearers of a new personality and character type. In the ideological throes of American triumphalism, postwar society was rapidly adopting a middle-class way of life that celebrated U.S. economic strength and a renewed sense of economic opportunity. For Whyte, however, an American

Dream identified with a middle-class lifestyle came at a cost. In addition to sacrificing their individuality to the organization, people in the new middle class encountered pressures to conform to an affluent lifestyle. "Fitting in" to one's leisure world largely meant "keeping up" with neighbors in a vast new suburban landscape where signs of material and social success were on display in the form of mass-produced goods.[16]

Mills, too, believed a huge price was being paid for the rewards of a middle-class way of life. Indeed, his landmark work, *White Collar* (1956), the classic sociological study of the makeup and character of the "new middle class," casts a long shadow over the newfound affluence and celebratory economic expansion of the 1950s. Perhaps his most ambitious and substantial achievement, this book brought together in one place a description of what many saw as disturbing trends in American life. Mills's primary focus was on change in the nature of work as seen in a massive expansion of a white-collar labor force precipitated by bureaucratic growth and the changing character of American business enterprise. More than merely a study of occupational change, Mills's book was also concerned with interconnections between the worlds of work and leisure as experienced by the armies of office workers, salespeople, salaried professionals, managers, supervisors, and others constituting the bulk of hired employees, people he called the "new little men."[17] More to the point, as his major study of social structure and character, *White Collar* was at bottom preoccupied with the problem of alienation. In Mills's view, the bureaucratic structures of the white-collar world led to a deskilling of jobs and a tedious, boring work experience to which the passive pleasures of mass culture were an impoverished compensatory response (what Theodor Adorno called "substitute gratification").[18] More significant than its effects on the economic class system, mass culture created *new forms* of alienation. On the one hand, deprived of a sense of self and identity at work, the new middle class exhibited "a psychology of prestige striving" in which feelings of self-worth, no longer part of the rewards of labor, were sought in the superfluous, consumerist-based signs of social status. On the other hand, the diversions of mass culture offered ultimately empty pleasure through manipulative, consumerist-oriented forms of entertainment. In both cases, Mills saw members of the new middle class as being denied meaningful and fulfilling lives through the bureaucratization of work and an emerging national culture of intellectually shallow, commercially packaged leisure pursuits.

Attempting both to update Marx's theory of alienation in work and market exchange and to draw on Weber's concept of bureaucracy, *White Collar* offers a provocative critique of middle-class society and character structure. Detracting from the book's strengths, however, is Mills's tendency to caricature the white-collar worker, a result of his failure to present a truly systematic and balanced analysis.[19] Mills stops short of looking at white-collar workers in the flesh, instead proffering speculative inferences from the structural and cultural features of the bureaucratic workplace and middle-class society. In spite of this methodological flaw, Mills's study still stands as a model of informed sociological investigation into the human problems of a bureaucratized capitalist society and culture.[20]

The Legacy of Postwar Social Criticism

The postwar critics cultivated a type of social analysis that put American society under a microscope for an educated mass readership. In doing so, they demonstrated the possibility of a grounded sociology that could engage an audience outside of academia. Journalistically inclined, these authors revived a critical analytical style reminiscent of Veblen and faithful to Lynd's call for a holistic approach to American culture.

At the same time, questions have abounded regarding the scientific status of this work. Some dismiss it out of hand as a form of "soft" social science failing the test of scientific rigor. While some grounds exist for this conclusion, it remains a somewhat biased and narrow judgment. With intellectual acumen and a medley of approaches and methods, these critics exhibited considerable investigative talents, skillfully connecting broad historical and cultural perspectives to a variety of observational research techniques. While their dependence on qualitative materials is cause for the displeasure of positivists, these critics were no strangers to quantitative data and used them when appropriate. Moreover, lest we forget that science means more than mere research methodology, the real significance of this work resides in its perceptive conceptualization of societal problems and its critical and theoretical insights into American life.

At the same time, there is no question as to the uneven quality of this work. Despite the attention given them by Mills, issues of power and inequality received only limited treatment by other writers. Understandably, the social and psychological effects of increasing abundance during this period seemed of greater importance to these writers than the concentration of power that emerged with the onset of the Cold War.[21] Also, these critics ignored inequities in the distribution of material resources, most notably the persistence of poverty behind the appearance of affluence. Cleavages in class structure and culture were mostly missing from the pictures they drew. Predating the civil rights and women's movements, these critics were relatively oblivious to issues of race, ethnicity, and gender. As middle-class white men living during a time of widespread upward mobility for urban and suburban whites, what they saw as problematic were issues of consumerism, suburbanization, and the plight of employees working in large organizations.

Additionally, while social character was one focus of attention, these writers failed to engage its study adequately. Lacking in-depth interviews and extensive participant observation, their depictions of changing social character and related psychological issues were often anecdotally based and relatively superficial and fragmentary.[22] Moreover, in most of these studies an analysis of character was limited to the impact of social structure and historical change on the individual while questions of agency went largely unaddressed.[23] Finally, while echoing many themes of the Frankfurt School, these critics' analyses might have been more penetrating had they appropriated theoretical tools and insights from these European scholars.

These omissions aside, postwar social criticism was groundbreaking for its portraits of the cultural and psychological characteristics of American society following the war. Abiding by the Millsian technique of taking historical social structure as context, these critics' broad field of vision enabled them to link evolving character and personality traits to "macro" social developments. Their work sought to characterize and question the institutional and cultural patterns and corresponding character types that were emerging in the changing worlds of work and leisure. These writers employed a comprehensive critical method of identifying and analyzing problems along two dimensions of these worlds: the material/economic and the cultural. While recognizing the primacy of material growth in the shaping of postwar life, these authors framed their views of change in cultural and social-psychological terms. They saw the main drift of values and beliefs as a function of individuals' adaptation to the group pressures accompanying materialistic lifestyles and bureaucratic organization.

More importantly, these critics' insights resonated with some enduring themes of modern social theory. First and foremost, implicit in this work is an extended discourse on the consequences of a weakening of traditional institutions, such as the family, religion, and community, as modern society shifts power and influence from these "primary" structures to the "secondary" structures of state and economy. These critics rightly saw bureaucratically organized patterns of work and leisure as overtaking communal influences and self-determined decision making among individuals and small groups. Postwar social criticism was thus rich in the cultural and psychological implications of the inroads of modern capitalism into daily life and the resulting difficulties facing those who would resist this powerful influence.

Second, if we were to identify a topical pattern in this body of work, it would most likely be its sustained commentary on problems of alienation and esteem. The pairing of these concepts is most apparent in Mills's *White Collar,* which while preoccupied with new forms of alienation also addressed what Mills perceived as the psychic burden attached to the quest for social esteem outside of work.[24] Indeed, the concept of alienation, with its sociological genesis in the early writings of Marx, and the concept of esteem, derivative of Weber's writings on status and status group, are thematized among all the social critics of this era. As historical social psychology, this work brought critical focus to the relationship between changing social and character structure, examining the connections between alienation as an "objective" problem of structure (although Mills also talked about alienation in terms of "feelings" of powerlessness) and esteem as a "subjective" problem of self and identity. Although the interplay of these Marxist and Weberian themes is most obvious in Mills, it is implicit in the work of Riesman, Whyte, and other authors of the time who saw social conformity as a loss of individuality and an estrangement from self.

Finally, it is worth noting the similarities between the postwar focus on alienation and esteem and the earlier writings of Veblen.[25] While concentrating on issues of esteem, Veblen touched on the problem of alienation in his comments on the contradiction between the socially cooperative demands of a machine-based economy and the predatory ways of capitalism.[26] Though primarily a social critic, given Veblen's familiarity with anthropology, economics, and history, the nature and scope of his work invite comparison to the classic theorists, including not only Marx and Weber but also Durkheim.

With the exception of Mills's work, American social criticism from the 1950s and 1960s is now largely forgotten but nonetheless remains an impressive and still relevant body of social science writings. While many of the issues have changed, these writers identified a set of core sociocultural problems that remain pertinent today. Though the content may be dated, this literature continues to be a model of publicly accessible critical social inquiry. A response to Lynd's and Mills's call for a pertinent social science, this work provides concrete, comprehensive, and comprehensible sociological accounts of a changing society and culture. As such, this genre continues to offer a compelling alternative to the overspecialized and formalist studies of the disciplinary mainstream of today.[27]

3

The Social Pragmatism of John Dewey

The pursuit of scientific respectability that shaped sociology during the 1940s and 1950s was followed in the 1960s by a strong reaction against this trend. Resembling an insurgency, this reaction manifested itself in a proliferation of new theories, methods, and research agendas that challenged the postwar orthodoxy of positivism and functionalism. The search for alternatives was driven largely by a growing perception of the discipline's lack of pertinence to major events and issues of the day, specifically the social unrest and cultural upheavals of that decade. The attempt to establish a regime of functionalism and quantitative research was thus countered by demands for different kinds of sociological inquiry reflective of the realities of contemporary American life. Opponents of the mainstream turned to Marxist sociology, the Frankfurt School, feminism and gender studies, phenomenological sociology, and eventually cultural studies, new French theory (poststructuralism, postmodernism), and neocolonial theory. Within the mainstream, numerous scholars shifted their attention to conflict theory, declaring it a more viable model of society than functionalism.[1] These alternative perspectives, constituting a new heterodoxy, represented a refusal of positivist science, system building, and mechanistic modes of explanation in favor of historically oriented, critical approaches focused on issues of inequality, power, subjectivity, and identity.[2]

The overall impact of these developments, however, has remained ambiguous. Although they brought new energy to the field, turning it in a more critical and "inclusive" direction, these movements failed to reverse the trend toward specialization and a fragmentation of the field into piecemeal approaches. Often drawn toward abstract theory, the bulk of these innovations lacked sociological substance. Perhaps worse, in a kind of disciplinary co-optation, the more important of these movements were converted into new subfields, further fragmenting the field. By offering their own particular perspectives, methodologies, and critical insights, this wide-ranging opposition fell short of constituting a new sociological vision of the kind advocated by Lynd in *Knowledge for What?* (1939) and Mills in *The Sociological Imagination* (1961). Moreover, the anti-Eurocentric and antiwhite male stance of many of these tendencies, fueled by the rise of what came to be called "identity politics," undermined the credibility of major sources of sociological alternatives to formalism, namely, the early Chicago researchers and the classic European theorists, all of whom were white men. By focusing on specific sociocultural categories and groups, identity politics led to new divisions in the field based on narrow preoccupations with group-based theoretical and political agendas. In sum, despite enriching sociology through their critiques, these reactive tendencies were unable to coalesce around a genuinely new paradigm, leaving the discipline even further dispersed and bereft of a common rationale and sense of purpose.

Reorientation: Philosophical Origins of Mills's Sociology

In contrast to these attempts at renewal, C. Wright Mills's proposals for a historical and structural focus on the individual constituted a model of a critical, multidimensional social analysis implying genuine change in the field. His work exemplified a creative theoretical and methodological stance and, perhaps more importantly, *a certain way of thinking about and doing sociology* that imparted intellectual, human, and political significance to the enterprise.

Mills's importance in this respect resides less in his own accomplishments, impressive as they were, than in the overall character and underlying presuppositions of his work. The most elemental of these are to be found primarily in the source both of Mills's early writings and his larger sociological vision and practice, namely, the philosophy of pragmatism. A former philosophy student, Mills was intimately acquainted with this philosophy, the subject of his doctoral dissertation in sociology.[3] From the very beginning, pragmatism shaped his intellectual disposition, directly contributing to his early work on social psychology and the sociology of knowledge and indirectly influencing his later work. The underlying motive force and character of Mills's thinking can thus be grasped and appreciated by examining its pragmatist origins. In short, pragmatism provided the philosophical moorings of the kind of sociology Mills advocated and practiced.[4]

The mode of inquiry Mills and the other postwar critics inherited from Thorstein Veblen contained a strong pragmatist element, namely, a questioning attitude toward existing reality. This feature of pragmatism contributed to the philosophical and intellectual underpinnings of Mills's uniquely provocative and down-to-earth work. Pragmatism was thus the context of Veblen's impact on Mills (Tilman 1984) and the connecting link between Mills and the other critics of his time. This philosophy pointed Mills in a direction that, when combined with classical social theory, gave his brand of sociology its critical intellectual energy, range, and depth.

The post–World War II social criticism discussed in Chapter 2 offers concrete examples of a type of sociological inquiry that avoids the limitations and perils of formalistic sociology. The search for an alternative to formalism, however, ultimately leads us further back historically, past the postwar social critics and Veblen to the latter's contemporaries in the pragmatist movement. In looking backward, we find that pragmatism's outlook on and way of understanding the world and human behavior have crucial implications for a transformation of sociology into a different kind of discipline. By extension, the basic principles and forms of reasoning and inquiry developed by the pragmatists, culminating in John Dewey, provide an overall theory, method, and raison d'être for more substantive and consequential forms of practice in all the social sciences.

Formalism on Trial

Having acquired multiple meanings, the term "pragmatism" immediately poses problems of definition. With origins in both nineteenth-century American life and the philosophers who gave it intellectual currency, scientific ground, and a public presence—Charles Sanders Peirce, William James, and John Dewey—this philosophy has been subject to numerous interpretations. As an innovative body of outlooks, ideas, arguments, and claims, pragmatist thinking has circulated widely among philosophers in the English-speaking world, manifesting itself in a variety of ways in a range of contexts. Enlarged and enriched over the years, the pragmatist challenge to philosophical tradition has nonetheless left an uncertain legacy.

In the writings of its originators, pragmatism comprises a more or less identifiable if not always consistent set of ideas, principles, and pictures of the world. What was distinctive and unifying about the views of its founders, however, was their opposition to formalistic modes of thought. Joining a host of similar thought movements, all of which, according to Morton White (1947), were in revolt against formalism, early pragmatism represented a sea change in Western philosophy involving a rejection of traditional metaphysics along with unending skepticism toward all ideas claiming a priori or universal status. In White's words:

> Pragmatism, instrumentalism, institutionalism, economic determinism, and legal realism exhibit striking philosophical kinships. They are all suspicious of approaches that are excessively formal; they all protest their anxiety to come to grips

> with reality, their attachment to the moving and vital in social life. (1947, 6)

Arising from a common intellectual ferment, the intent of these movements was to disclaim all formal and abstract modes of thought. These movements stood for direct engagement with the problems posed by a social world of dynamic change and development, a world that could be grasped only from the perspective of modern empirical science. All of these movements, according to White, "insist[ed] on coming to grips with life, experience, process, growth, context, function" (1947, 13).

In one interpretation, this novel way of thinking was less a product of internal developments in the field of philosophy than of external events. John Patrick Diggins (1994) argues that pragmatism took shape as a distinct philosophy at a time of cultural and spiritual crisis in American life. This was a crisis of authority precipitated by modern science and industry, forces perceived as threatening the traditional beliefs and values of rural, small-town America. For many thinkers, especially William James, it was mainly religion and spiritual life that were endangered by the modernist outlook promulgated by technology, big capitalism, and rapid change. For Dewey and others, modernism meant a potential crisis in human values generally, a crisis calling for an expanded conception of science able to reconcile the scientific worldview with cherished and sacred beliefs.

Although James and Dewey saw a need to protect the realm of belief and value from the desacralizing effects of science, their pragmatism was in a sense a *modern* response to modernism. These men saw pragmatism as fundamentally scientific in nature and as promoting new habits of thought, attitudes, and social practices capable of accommodating science to the lay world of human values, a reconciliation they felt was crucial for social progress and the general welfare. Democratically minded and suspicious of vested interests, the early pragmatists were motivated by a conviction that philosophy should join with modern science and technology to address the needs of the entire society. This meant overcoming the isolation of science from the public through the formation of a democratic community of scientists producing knowledge serving the common good.

Situating Pragmatism

There is a common perception that pragmatism is a philosophy of "practicality" based on the criterion of "what works" and that this habit of thought has deep roots in American soil. Such a view challenges Diggins's interpretation of pragmatism as a response to modernization. Regardless of the extent to which a "pragmatic" frame of mind informing daily life existed prior to extensive modernization, "what works" is hardly an accurate rendering of pragmatist philosophy. While the common narrative that equates "pragmatic" with "practical" has its place, the view that pragmatism is a philosophy of practical results, or simple utilitarianism, is a gross misinterpretation of the work of Peirce, James, and Dewey. Rather, these men formulated a way of thinking that could be called a "philosophy of consequences."

Situating pragmatism on the historical and intellectual map can be daunting, given its multiple origins and overlap with other thought movements of the time.[5] In today's context, although seemingly unlikely, it is useful to compare pragmatism to philosophical postmodernism.[6] That the neopragmatism of Richard Rorty, Hilary Putman, Richard Bernstein, and others should emerge from the "postmodern turn" suggests a certain affinity between the two philosophies. First, both pragmatism and contemporary postmodern philosophy reject absolutes, universals, foundations, final causes, and other conventional features of traditional metaphysics and monistic thinking, much of which the postmodernist Jean-François Lyotard captured in his phrase "master narratives" (1984). Both philosophies exhibit strong pluralizing tendencies, and both regard "truth" as always provisional, based on the principle of fallibilism. Second, both pragmatism and postmodernism are in different but overlapping ways representations of a sensibility reflecting a democratization of culture, understood as an attitudinal trend of openness and inclusiveness often associated with American ideals and manners. That these philosophies were from the beginning so closely connected to their social and historical contexts, giving changing circumstances, perceptions, and sentiments theoretical expression, is itself testimony to a weakening of barriers between intellectual elites and the wider populace, a significant indicator of social and cultural democratization.[7] Dewey understood democracy as a necessary condition for and outcome of the realization of his philosophy, while the writings of American postmodernists exhibit strong antielitist and antihierarchical views. Thus, we find in both pragmatism and postmodernism democratic proclivities and an underlying populist spirit.

While this comparison offers a suggestive framing of pragmatism in the intellectual and cultural scheme of things, looking at pragmatism from this angle should not detract from its pre-postmodernist impact on numerous areas of twentieth-century thought. A "generic pragmatism" based on the basic philosophical premises of its originators has appeared not only among some postmodernists but also in the teachings of George Herbert Mead, Ludwig Wittgenstein, Herbert Blumer, and a number of analytical philosophers, not to mention its impact on a generation of mid-twentieth-century public intellectuals.[8]

Philosophical Revolt

For the purpose of exploring pragmatism's implications for sociology and its connections to the work of Mills, it is sufficient to extract only the salient ideas of its founders, particularly those of John Dewey. The pertinence of Dewey for a rehabilitation of sociology begins with the strong antiformalist tendencies in his thought. While maintaining a firm commitment to scientific thinking, moreover, Dewey's intellectual perspective and his conception of inquiry run counter to the basic premises of positivism, an anchor of sociological formalism.

What I call Dewey's "social pragmatism" is suggestive of a sociological practice characterized by (1) direct engagement with substantive societal problems, (2) theory and research serving the public good, (3) recognition and accounting of the social origins and character of knowledge, and (4) an approach to social inquiry in which positivist methods play a limited role alongside methodological protocols more germane to the requirements of the subject matter. Traceable to Dewey's writings, these are cardinal features of Mills's work that provide a fresh appreciation from a pragmatist perspective of the substance and spirit of his sociological project.

In Louis Menand's view, pragmatism was reducible to what he called an *attitude.* More to the point, this philosophy was based not on a set of ideas but rather on

> only a single idea—an idea about ideas. [These thinkers] believed that ideas are not "out there" waiting to be discovered but are tools . . . that people devise to cope with the world in which they find themselves. They believed that ideas are produced . . . by groups of individuals—that they are social. . . . [I]deas do not develop according to some inner logic of their own but are entirely dependent . . . on their human carriers and the environment. . . . [S]ince ideas are provisional responses to particular and unreproducible circumstances, their survival depends not on their immutability but on their adaptability. (2001, xi–xii)

In fact, this characterization of pragmatist philosophy suggests much more than adoption of a mere attitude but indicates an approach to ideas and knowledge that changes the nature of philosophy itself, namely its grounding in concrete reality and the everyday problems of ordinary human beings. The pragmatists, in effect, redefined philosophy, changing it from being a means to *truth,* a notion they repeatedly questioned, to being a *guide* to thought and action. In this respect, it would seem that Menand's claim that pragmatism sees ideas merely as "tools" is an oversimplification of what is actually an intricate and comprehensive theory of the relationship of ideas to human experience and practice.

Though a highly original conception of the nature of knowledge was the unifying thread of pragmatism's three major founders, there were significant differences among them with respect to the form this conception took and how it was to be developed. As the most scientifically oriented member of the group and the inventor of the term "pragmatism," Charles Sanders Peirce claimed that "knowing" was dependent not on philosophical reflection but rather an ongoing process of inquiry that was social in nature. Formulating a set of logical and epistemological principles governing this process, Peirce from the beginning gave pragmatism a scientific foundation through a body of reasoning and rules regarding how to practice philosophy in a genuinely knowing yet provisional way. Most important was his formulation of the famous "pragmatic maxim." This was a succinct statement about the nature of concepts that was to serve as the central premise of pragmatist thought. According to this maxim, "the meaning of a concept is a matter of the practical effects of acting in accordance with it" (Bacon 2012, 3).[9] For Peirce, "practical" had a broad meaning connoting "practice"; in other words, our concepts and ideas were to be understood in terms of their outcomes in the context of actual human practices. In this view, concepts in some sense literally "mean" their real effects in and on life. This is the original formulation of the foundational pragmatist notion that thought and knowledge are to be understood and judged according to their consequences in the real world. Concepts and practices are thus part of a unity of human action.[10]

The better-known writings of William James exhibit some continuity with Peirce's groundbreaking work but contain a provocative twist on the maxim. James complicates the maxim by arguing that the meaning of an idea or proposition depends on the psychological effects of believing in its truth (Talisse and Aiken 2008, 13). The notion of *belief* thus becomes a central theme in James's version of pragmatism (see James 1955, 1985). This move in turn is an aspect of James's introduction of the notion of *experience* into the pragmatist lexicon and a refocusing of the maxim on the psychological and subjective dimensions of the individual. By these means James effectively redefines the consequences of thought in terms of what people come to believe as a result of their own personal experiences and how this translates psychologically into their view of the world and themselves. This conception is most apparent in James's *The Va-*

rieties of Religious Experience (1985), a study in the psychology of religious and spiritual belief.[11] James's psychologizing of the pragmatist theory of truth has both endeared him to a wide reading public and brought charges of an overly subjective and relativizing conception of the maxim.[12] By turning to experience, James shifted emphasis to questions of epistemology and empirical verification, preparing the ground for a radical critique of traditional empiricism. According to James, the traditional empiricists (read "British empiricists") held an atomistic view of the universe, in the words of Richard Bernstein, mistakenly seeing "experience as consisting of the aggregate of discrete units." We know this view to be false, James argued, because "we have *direct* experience of the connections, relations, and transitions within the direct flow of experience" (Bernstein 2010, 57; italics in original).[13] It is through our own experience of the world, then, that we are able to discern the real nature of things and their evolving interrelationships. James thus developed a pragmatism predicated on a person-centered epistemology that privileged direct experience over analytical categories and formal methods of inquiry.[14] Insisting, in pragmatist anti-Cartesian fashion, on the inseparability of impressions and ideas (ibid., 56), James rejected both atomistic descriptions of the phenomenal world and intellectual abstractions, claiming concrete experience as the source of knowledge and the ground of guided action.

Behind these differences was a consensus among the three thinkers that was the basis of their modus operandi: philosophy was in dire need of reconstruction. For Peirce, this meant giving philosophy a scientific foundation, and for James it meant subordinating philosophy to psychology and the repository of human experience. Building on these views, Dewey felt reconstruction meant a thoroughgoing critique of traditional philosophy, involving a new set of presuppositions and categories and the formulation of new principles and concepts. Accordingly, Dewey systematically developed an original and comprehensive philosophy with implications for the full range of human knowledge and activity, including psychology, society, politics, education, logic, science, art, ethics, and morality. While he generously credited Peirce and James for opening new doors, Dewey effectively turned pragmatism into a socially oriented, highly textured philosophy of exceptional range.

Dewey's Reconstruction Project

The problems of interpretation associated with Dewey's writings stem in part from a lack of clarity and consistency in his work. However, many of the difficulties in understanding Dewey result from the originality and subtlety of his thinking as well as the challenges posed by the task of reconstructing philosophy in a wholesale manner. Dewey's tireless efforts to change the character of philosophical thought meant that his formulations often stretched the limits of conventional language and accepted philosophical discourse. Difficulty in interpreting Dewey also is aggravated by the sheer scope and volume of his work and the fact that in the course of his long life his work evolved through a number of phases.[15]

Dewey sought incessantly to change not *what* we think but *how* we think. This is apparent in his open dislike of the Western propensity to categorize and compartmentalize and his persistent emphasis on the interrelatedness and interdependence of everything in the physical and social universes. Of special import for social science and social theory, Dewey was a unifier. A strong believer in "the unity of knowledge" (Menand 2001, 322), he was dismayed by modernity's tendencies toward specialization and abstraction, as manifested in the differentiation of culture into distinct and separate realms.[16] Against this trend, Dewey pursued a holistic philosophy geared to the problems of everyday life and aimed at removing what he regarded as artificial barriers among different spheres of thought and action. At the same time, rejecting traditional metaphysics, Dewey abhorred all dualisms—subject-object, mind-body, theory-practice, fact-value, science-morality, art-life, and so forth. These are focal points of Dewey's antiformalism and his resolve to transform philosophy from contemplative reflection into an integrated, practical, and grounded method of engagement with the concrete problems of life.

The reach, complexity, and passion of Dewey's efforts were destined to result in an imposing but ambiguous legacy. Given the ambitiousness of his project, there are grounds to judge Dewey as having failed to reach his goal. Yet to this day, Dewey is widely regarded as the leading pragmatist thinker and most important figure in twentieth-century American thought. Indeed, one difficulty facing any discussion of pragmatism is the fact that many ideas and principles of the original thinkers, primarily Peirce and Dewey, have been widely assimilated in various fields of knowledge.

Many of Dewey's writings take the form of a critique of traditional philosophy. In a more positive vein, Dewey saw his own philosophy as a worldview and method appropriate to the problems of modern life and consistent with the outlook of modern science. In regarding Dewey from a more affirmative perspective, however, we encounter a recurring problem. Dewey's writings exhibit the same quality of interrelatedness that he saw in the world. It is virtually impossible to grasp the precise import of any one of Dewey's claims or concepts without examining all of them simultaneously. Dewey's metaphysics, logic, psychology, educational theory, social thought, and politics are so thoroughly intertwined that an understanding of any part of his philosophy depends on or is closely conditioned by knowledge of the other parts. Finally, it helps matters to allow room for Dewey's polemical style and method, bearing in mind that the negative tone of much of his writing is a by-product of his tenacious critique of pre-Darwinian philosophy.

Deserving of greater attention than the scientific side of pragmatism, however, are the claims of Peirce and Dewey concerning the *social* foundations of knowledge. As a semiotician, Peirce had already given mental life a social cast in his theories of communication and the sign. As Bernstein notes, "Peirce argues that all language, signification, and consequently all inquiry and its end product, knowledge, are essentially social in character" (1999, 176). This became the central principle grounding Dewey's metaphysical assumptions and the basis of his belief in the intrinsic connections among science, education, and democracy. According to Dewey, the quest for knowledge through experimental inquiry is always undertaken within a context of social meanings and relations and within a community of actors. Dewey's insights into the social basis of ideas and inquiry were the source of a distinctive approach to the problem of knowledge and his most important contribution to our understanding of the purpose and practice of philosophy and science.

Indeed, as Mills discerned, by making the social foundation of human intelligence a key principle of his theorizing, Dewey established a basis for a sociology of knowledge. Despite its obvious pertinence to social science and social theory, Dewey's conception of the social character of thought and knowledge has never been adequately explored or appreciated. The weight Dewey placed on the social has two aspects. First, it implies that all scientific inquiry should be approached in terms of its social foundations and those of its objects of inquiry. The prominence of the social in Dewey's philosophy even suggests that, for him, a sociology-of-knowledge perspective would ideally be the frame of all sociological theory and research. Second, Dewey's belief in the social interconnectedness of all human activity, including mental activity, is a major source of his antipathy toward formalism, dualistic thinking, and excessive abstraction. Generally speaking, intimations in Dewey's thought of a broad-based sociology of knowledge offer the possibility of greater intellectual perspective and depth in the practice of all the social sciences.

An understanding of Dewey, especially for social scientists, is best achieved by focusing attention on the two concepts central to his philosophy and conception of science: *experience* and *inquiry*. Attuned to Peirce's rigorous arguments about scientific method, Dewey was preoccupied throughout his life with questions concerning the logic and nature of scientific inquiry. At the same time, Dewey seized on the emphasis James placed on experience, and it became the foundation of his conception of "the empirical" and for his critique of abstract, reflective philosophy and the positivist version of empiricism. Dewey's views of experience and inquiry were linked in the form of a biologically inflected "behaviorism" derived from Charles Darwin and shaped by Hegelian categories, a linking that became the basis of his conception of both science and social life.[17] While the recurring concern of Dewey's work was the conduct of inquiry (Mills 1964, 356), the notions of both inquiry and experience were the main weapons in Dewey's dispute with philosophical orthodoxy, laying the foundation for his view of action as intelligent adaptation to a changing environment. Dewey's point was that a mode of inquiry addressing real-life problems could be developed only within the context of experience and an understanding of our place in the natural world. In short, as Bernstein notes, "Dewey attempted to combine a new method for dealing with specific problems within a comprehensive theory of experience and nature" (Dewey 1960a, xviii).

Dewey on Experience

If Dewey has been a controversial figure it surely is not unrelated to his reliance on the concept of experience. As Martin Jay (2005) has demonstrated, the rich history of this concept provides abundant evidence of both its significance in Western thought and its problematic character. With the rise in modern society of individualism and a preoccupation with subjectivity, the concept of experience gained considerable currency, and it continues to have a conspicuous presence in contemporary discourse. Given its innate ambiguity and affinities with psychology, however, the philosophical viability of the concept has been repeatedly questioned.[18]

Dewey himself was aware of the difficulties with the concept of experience but regarded it as too valuable to abandon. Holding firm, he converted its murky meaning into a strategic advantage, employing the inherent ambiguity of the concept in an astute theoretical move. Following James, Dewey recognized that its "troublesome" double reference to that which is both subjective and objective—involving an *experiencer* and something *experienced*—made the concept of central importance to the pragmatist project of uniting subject and object. "Experience" served Dewey's goal of overcoming dualistic thinking in general and the gulf between idealism and realism in particular, essential features of Dewey's assault on traditional philosophy. In this respect, the concept was instrumental in redefining "the empirical" as involving simultaneously the active mental construction of phenomena on the part of knowers and the existence of an external world of observable "facts" and "events."

For Dewey, the concept of experience performed the critical function of situating philosophy in lived reality. As an indication of its importance to his philosophy, Dewey employed the notion in two notably different ways. In a metaphysical sense, experience was the ground of all thought, knowledge, and inquiry. As carefully laid out in his essay "The Need for a Recovery of Philosophy" (Dewey 1960a) and in *Experience and Nature* (Dewey 1958b), a transformation in philosophical method depended on acceptance of the proposition that, far from leading an autonomous existence, thought was "bound up" in the experience on which it reflected (Mills 1964, 364). As Dewey put it in *Reconstruction in Philosophy,* "Knowledge is not something separate and self-sufficing, but is involved in the process by which life is sustained and evolved" (1957, 87). In addition to this axiomatic use of the term, Dewey put forth a normative theory of experience. The concept takes on evaluative meaning in *Art as Experience* (Dewey 1958a), when Dewey postulates that the sense of consummation associated with aesthetic experience is the generic form of human fulfillment in all areas of life.

An appreciation of how Dewey arrived at his conception directs our attention to the genesis of his philosophical orientation. His early attraction to Georg Wilhelm Friedrich Hegel, he claims, was motivated by a "demand for unification" rooted in the isolating effects of "New England culture" (Dewey 1960a, 10). Initially, Dewey was attracted to the idea of the "organic" that Hegel had elevated to a universal category (ibid., xxi). The notion of the organic supported Dewey's growing belief in the principle of interrelatedness and served a vital purpose in his attack on what he believed were false dichotomies.

With Dewey's turn to the Darwinian theory of evolution, the organic became a biological category referring to the relationship between an organism and its environment. This relationship became a framework for much of Dewey's subsequent thinking, providing an image of the interconnectedness of things that was integral to what became his "naturalistic" theory.[19] According to Dewey, the social world exhibits certain generic traits common to nature. Life is full of activity, change, contingency—key features of Darwin's view of evolution in which processes of adaptation and structural differentiation account for the development of various species and their relationship to environing conditions. Not only did Dewey see Darwin's theory as descriptive of social life; Darwin's work also had implications for the application of scientific method to the study of human beings as biological and social creatures (Dewey 1965, v). Dewey's adoption of a Darwinian perspective was the beginning of his lifelong belief that solutions to the problems of society depended on an evolutionary perspective and more generally the concepts and methodologies of science.

Despite a gradual transition to Darwin, Dewey remained faithful to certain Hegelian ideas. This was facilitated by the concept of the organic, which linked the Hegelian and Darwinian dimensions of Dewey's thought. While ignoring elements of Hegel that seemed unproductive, Dewey's thinking continued to draw on basic Hegelian principles (Jay 2005, 288). As Dewey put it, "Acquaintance with Hegel has left a permanent deposit in my thinking" (Dewey 1960a, 12). From the standpoint of social theory, the enduring influence of Hegel is most apparent in the emphasis Dewey placed on the social character of knowledge and his understanding of the intersubjective foundation of the sociocultural world. Another Hegelian debt is apparent in the historicist dimension in Dewey, an important but underplayed feature of his view of social change that he often combined with the Darwinian conception to create a picture of "histories" within the workings of nature and society (Dewey 1958b, xii). While occasionally employing the organic concept in a biological sense, positing parallels and interconnections between nature and society, Dewey never completely abandoned Hegel's conception of the organic character of social and cultural evolution. Contextualizing problems in historically specific periods and conditions was a significant feature of Dewey's relativizing approach to knowledge and his method of moving from philosophical monism to the particulars of human history and the pluralistic character of society.

Relatedly, Hegel's propensity to totalize reappears in Dewey's drive to unify, perhaps most apparent in his view of society as a unity of differentiated but interconnected structures and functions seen as parts of a whole.

What has been called Dewey's "naturalized Hegelianism" enabled him to devise an integrated and dynamic approach to knowledge. He saw the concept of experience as the means by which philosophy could be rid of both the subject-object dichotomy and the well-known error of "misplaced concreteness" (Whitehead 1958, 52).[20] Dewey argues that experience is not just a matter of possessing knowledge but "an affair of the intercourse of a living being with its physical and social environment" (Dewey 1960a, 23). It follows that experience is not restricted to the category of subjectivity but designates a subject-object relationship based on functional distinctions in which an objective reality enters into the mental functioning of subjects and in turn is modified by their responses. Dewey states that experience is inherently empirical, full of particulars, but these particulars are tied together by all kinds of "connections and continuities" (ibid.). Contrary to the conventional belief that experience and thought are "antithetical," thought is *embedded* in and *emanates* from experience, which is in Dewey's words "full of inference" (ibid.). Reason is intrinsic to experience itself and thus inseparable from the life processes within which experience takes place.

By situating thought within the flow of experience, Dewey imparts to mental life an implicitly activist orientation. This was his means of rejecting the now widely disputed "spectator" and "copy" theories of knowledge, which treat the subject as a passive observer and recorder of "external" phenomena. The active and dynamic character of experience, and therefore thought, becomes explicit in what is perhaps Dewey's most consequential theoretical argument. He says that because most philosophies dwell in the past and the present, they have ignored the future, which is necessarily the preoccupation of a philosophy like pragmatism, as it is focused on consequences. Adopting a passive stance, traditional empiricisms have taken the past and present as a "given." But "experience in its vital form is experimental, an effort to *change the given;* it is characterized by projection" (1960a, 23; italics added). The experimental attitude that inheres in experience is future oriented, marked by "anticipation and prediction" (ibid., 63). Here, Dewey is framing pragmatism at its modernist best, showing how thought is now geared to activity and action and how these aspects of experience direct our attention to the future outcomes of present actions and events. In this respect, Dewey gives expression to a major strand of late modern philosophy, citing the importance of the *temporal* dimension of existence (ibid.) and incorporating it at the center of his theory.[21] Here we find an obvious parallel to Mead's ideas as presented especially in *The Philosophy of the Present* (1980), in which Mead underscores the temporal character of social life.[22] And temporality reappears in Herbert Blumer's (1969) exposition of symbolic interactionism, which places emphasis on the anticipatory nature of action and interaction. In Blumer's polemic, human behavior is accounted for less by causal explanations based on antecedent factors than by the forward pull arising from actors' interpretations and definitions of their situations.

Finally, it is important to stress how thoroughly Dewey defended the "naturalistic" character of his theory. The title of *Experience and Nature* was intended to closely link these concepts, as the contents of the book clearly reveal. Implying widespread resistance to the inclusion of nature in philosophical thought, Dewey comments, "In the natural sciences there is a union of experience and nature which is not greeted as a monstrosity" (1958b, 2a). Elsewhere he states, "Experience is *of* as well as *in* nature" (ibid, 4a; italics in original). Although the context of this statement clearly indicates that Dewey is saying that nature is *what* we experience, "*of*" in this instance bears a double meaning that should not be lost on readers. Dewey's line of reasoning suggests that experience and thus knowledge somehow *embody* nature. In either interpretation, he clearly posits experience as *rooted* in nature, thus claiming their inseparability. While Dewey does not make sufficiently clear what he includes in the category "nature," we can reasonably infer that, viewed from a Darwinian perspective, Dewey intends "nature" as a reference to human existence as a whole, with primary emphasis on the similarities between biological and social life. For him, these are comparable in character and intimately intertwined within the realm of experience.[23]

Dewey on Inquiry

For Dewey, a viable theory of inquiry depended on a radically transformed conception of the nature of logic. Dewey's writings on this topic are so unorthodox that they are probably "the hardest to understand, even for the professional logician" (Hook 1995, 88). This fact bears a certain irony, considering that Dewey apparently was preoccupied with questions of logic and inquiry throughout his career. Fortunately, by contextualizing his remarks within the larger project of pragmatism, it is possible to grasp his basic position and intent.

We can best understand Dewey's theory by first seeing it as an attempt to disavow traditional arguments in epistemology. These he dismisses as a wasteful diversion perpetuated by formal logic and adherence to outmoded philosophical conceptions. As a counterpoint to what he considers epistemological dead ends, Dewey draws our attention to the *function* of logic. Beginning with the Greeks, logic has traditionally been a formal system of abstract, universally valid rules of reasoning. By contrast, Dewey defines logic as a set of mental operations tied to *controlled empirical inquiry.* Once logic's function in inquiry is properly understood, he argues, we can dispense with the insoluble problems of traditional theories of knowledge, and logic can assume its proper role as a component of experimental inquiry based on systematic observation.

As suggested by the title of his voluminous work *Logic: The Theory of Inquiry*, for Dewey logic is not a matter of abstract reasoning or a set of a priori formal rules imposed on thinking from the outside but rather an essential part of the act of inquiry. According to Dewey, "All logical forms (with their characteristic properties) arise within the operation of inquiry and are concerned with control of inquiry so that it may yield warranted assertions" (2013, 13). These forms "*originate*" (ibid.; italics in original) in the process of inquiry itself, emerging from within investigations into the concrete problems for which we seek solutions. While Dewey seems to be rejecting all inherited conceptions, from the sound of his statement it would be a mistake to assume that his view consists of a complete rejection of basic Aristotelian logic. Rather, he seems to be saying that logic is not completely fixed in advance but is conditioned and shaped in practice in the course of a particular inquiry. Logic may involve accepted principles or rules of reasoning, but when employed in inquiry these vary in meaning, application, and consequences, depending on the practical purposes they serve in resolving an actual problem at hand, in all its contingencies. Inquiry is the context of logic; logic thus takes form in the process of inquiry.

As with many of his ideas, it is important to grasp the *functional* character of Dewey's conception. While he does not always make the distinction apparent, Dewey sees logic as performing both "descriptive and prescriptive" functions (Bernstein 1966, 102). Logic is a strategy both of ascertaining how inquiry is actually conducted and of evaluating its procedures. Since inquiry is an observable act that can be "objectively" studied, "the function of logic is to discern methods and patterns of inquiry in order to provide us with a guide to better and more successful inquiries" (ibid.). Logic's purpose, thus, is to bring about continual improvements in how we engage in the processes of discovery and knowledge production, thereby increasing our likelihood of achieving desired ends. Dewey is effectively drawing a contrast between formal logic and logic-in-use, equating the latter to operations and procedures the purpose of which is to clarify and assess the methods and consequences of inquiry as actually practiced.

Dewey's focus on the practical functionality of logic in experimental discovery underscores the pragmatist idea that mental functions are enmeshed in the activity of life itself. Logic is an instrument of the intellect embedded in our efforts to investigate, understand, and cope with the environment in which we live and act. Logic is a guide to action. More than a predetermined or principled set of abstract norms standing on their own, logic is integral to our experience of life and refracts the processes involved in discovering what we know of our world. Linking logic to reason and rationality, and in one of his characteristic warnings about the dangers of abstraction, Dewey strives to ground logic in practical activity in his claim that "reasonableness or rationality has . . . been hypostasized" (2013, 23). Here, Dewey invokes the pragmatist concern for the relationship between means and ends, the basic framework within which all human activity, including thought, is to be defined and appraised.[24] Insofar as it is an essential element of what we call reason, or rationality, logic is thus inherently practical and adaptive in character. As Dewey put it, "Rationality is an affair of the relation of *means and consequences,* not of fixed first principles as ultimate premises" (ibid., 22; italics in original).

Dewey's view of the connection of logic to inquiry has considerable significance in terms of his overall philosophy and in this respect conveys, like all of his ideas, an important set of social meanings. First of all, it is apparent that logic is social in nature, insofar as inquiry is socially conditioned and situated. Logic is an integral part of scientific reasoning, which, as Peirce pointed out, is part of a social process occurring within a group or community of inquirers. Second, logic as an evaluative guide to the practice of inquiry is no longer to be considered as merely a conceptual operation but a form of action.[25] Third, and most important, inquiry fulfills a purpose beyond empirical discovery and knowledge production: it is an act of *problem solving,* the very heart of Dewey's philosophy. For him, the primary function of our capacity for reason is the overcoming of problems encountered in the course of living.

Inquiry, thus, is *motivated* by a need to solve problems, and logic is a mode or quality of thought that reflects and serves the requirements of such inquiry. In Dewey's conception, logic is a kind of diagnostic mode of analysis intended to evaluate the consequences of methodical efforts at problem resolution. Intelligent/scientific thinking leads to inquiry as a problem-solving instrument; in turn, the consequences of inquiry shape intelligent thought around the most workable strategy for solving problems, resulting in a revision of procedures and operations.

A number of important points follow from this account. First of all, it is clear that *inquiry as problem solving* is the central philosophical theme of Deweyan thought, around which most of his major conceptions "cluster" (Mills 1964, 356). Second, and closely related, the extensive attention Dewey gives to inquiry illustrates how, as Mills says, "Dewey's analysis of '*thinking*' constitutes the foundation of his thought" (ibid.; italics added).[26] Third, Dewey's detailed treatment of inquiry is indicative of the weight he gives to *methodology* in the pragmatists' approach to science and specifically reflects the profound influence of Peirce in Dewey's thinking. Fourth, it is apparent that Dewey conceives of inquiry as a form of *action*. The purpose of inquiry is to change a problematic situation into one that is "workable," in which doubts, tensions, conflicts, needs, and so on are resolved. Fifth, his conception of logic as a set of operations inseparable from the concrete act of inquiry is a manifestation of Dewey's vigorous rejection of dualistic thinking. Inquiry involves a unification of subject and object, theory and practice, in a continuum of mental and physical activity that proceeds within a single, indivisible structure of discovery. Indeed, Dewey's battle against dualism is in a sense most tangibly waged in his strategy of removing logic from the realm of abstract reasoning and relocating it within the precincts of worldly investigation.

It is apparent that Dewey's treatment of logic represents a decisive statement of pragmatist methodology as a reasoned, empirical, situation-based, and methodical approach to problem solving.[27] More generally, as a fundamental revision of conventional thinking about the nature of logic, Dewey's arguments convey his conviction that thought and theory are forms of action and therefore have real and tangible consequences in our lives. In this sense, his theory gives expression to the pragmatist project of approaching both thought and action from the standpoint of their actual consequences in the stream of human experience and in terms of how they serve to further the realization of desired human ends.[28]

Dewey on Science

Despite the contribution of Dewey's theory of inquiry to our understanding of pragmatist philosophy, the generic nature of his conception raises a number of questions. For one thing, there are many kinds, or types, of inquiry, each of which involves a different set of conditions and circumstances. For another, Dewey's "inquiry" is a slippery concept, bearing multiple shades of meaning in relation to the gamut of Dewey's many concerns. As Mills observes, "Some of the surrogates and synonyms of 'inquiry' are 'thought' . . . 'science,' . . . 'reflection,' . . . 'method,' . . . 'intelligence'" (Mills 1964, 357). In this respect, Dewey's strategy of conceptual unification and interlinking of different dimensions and domains of thought runs the risk of imprecision and confusion.

These are significant difficulties when it comes to interpreting Dewey's view of science. As Mills comments, "Dewey's theory of 'inquiry' is allegedly 'empirical.' What does this mean?" (1964, 357). Mills considers a number of possibilities while pointing out that Dewey's statements about the interconnections of observable phenomena fail to address the question of what *kind* of evidence counts as "empirical," and in relation to what particular types of subject matter.

This problem has a close bearing on the question of Dewey's position on positivism. At first glance, his recurring appeals to the natural sciences suggest that he regards them as a model of science in general, placing him in the positivist camp. There is a definite antipositivist thrust, however, in Dewey's insistence on the continuity of science with other forms and fields of thought, particularly what he calls "common sense." This could be taken to mean that he does not see the natural sciences as representing *the* model of scientific inquiry, as the positivists do, and that inquiry takes many forms along a continuum from intelligent thinking in the everyday world to controlled laboratory experiments. Dewey, moreover, in his later years engaged in "long and vigorous debate" with the logical positivists (Tilman 2004, 236), a further indication of his antipositivist disposition. Perhaps most conclusively, Dewey's theory of *experience* as the ground of discovery and test of knowledge is entirely inconsistent with the positivist belief in a world of sense data independent of the mental constructions of the observer. Dewey's refusal of the dichotomous opposition of subject and object and related dualisms effectively eliminates the gap between the world of "facts" and the mind of the scientist. For Dewey, facts are a product of human perception and cognition and meaningless in the absence of valuation (see Chapter 5). The positivist attempt to separate sense data from the subjective and social factors affecting how these data are constructed conceptually is for Dewey also entirely unwarranted. Finally, in an antipositivist protest against the absolute authority of the natural sciences, Dewey states, "The assimilation of human science to physical science represents . . . only another form of absolutistic logic, a kind of physical absolutism" (Dewey 1954, 199).[29]

Yet, when we consider how Dewey might distinguish between the natural and social sciences, his position on positivism would appear to be more nuanced. Dewey's repeated appeals to the natural sciences indicate that he conflated them with the social sciences and imply that all types of inquiry must conform to the rules and procedures of the former. This seems to be the way Mills saw the matter, as he said that "Dewey's statement and location of *scientific method* tends to be controlled by *biological* considerations" (Mills 1964, 384; italics in original).[30] But while for Dewey the "natural sciences" means primarily biology, he understands this in terms of Darwin's model of organism and environment, which immediately introduces a social dimension and the notion of an active subject. Dewey puts forth Darwinian biology as a *model for thinking* about the organic character of social relations and social inquiry, not as a definition of the nature of the subject matter and methods appropriate to it. Drawing on the model of biology, Dewey's theory of experience strives, as we've seen, to "naturalize" the social world. As a basic life science and the field Darwin made famous, biology provides Dewey with a set of *principles* in terms of which he characterizes the adaptive and emergent character of knowledge and society. At the level of investigation, the biological model provides the framework within which Dewey outlines his theory of inquiry as problem solving, a theory that clearly presupposes a Darwinian conception of adaptation through action and purposive change. The actual procedures of inquiry serve a Darwinian purpose insofar as they generate solutions to situational problems. Dewey thus sees inquiry as performing adaptive functions, regardless of content or subject matter, and thus serving a necessary scientific and practical purpose independently of any *particular* methodological or analytical approach. This obviously leaves some room for the techniques and models of natural science without necessarily excluding interpretive methods.

Indeed, there is ample evidence that Dewey and, following him, Mills, believed that selection of a mode of inquiry should be determined by its appropriateness to a given problem, and it is apparent that this principle applies to subject matter itself. Consistent with Aristotle, Dewey recognized that "different subject matters require different rules of procedure" (Bernstein, in Dewey 1960a, xxxi). This "methodological pragmatism" (Tilman 2004, 258) contextualized inquiry situationally, which in today's terms means a commitment to methodological pluralism. Viewed from this angle, Dewey's arguments about science and inquiry would not necessarily preclude the use of positivist methods. The generality and openness of his conception of inquiry should thus be construed as allowing for both interpretive and positivist types of sociological theory and research. In this sense, despite his opposition to the positivist movement, Dewey would likely have endorsed both "meaningful" and "positivist" types of explanation, without necessarily advocating one over the other. The most plausible interpretation of Dewey's position would thus seem to be that he opposed the *reduction* of science to the positivist paradigm.

Finally, Dewey's generic conception conveys a picture of inquiry, and therefore science, as being a form of what we might call "everyday methodology." Despite its institutionalization as a body of specialized knowledge, science in his view is not—or *should* not be—an isolated, esoteric enclave detached from the rest of life, arrogating to itself absolute authority on factual and explanatory matters. Resisting this kind of elitism, Dewey believed that (1) science is rooted in the same *capacities* for intelligence and problem solving that we all share as human beings and (2) its findings have *consequences* beyond the specialized, institutional confines of professional scientific fields. By the same token, the controlled procedures of scientific inquiry should serve as a model for thinking in everyday life, or "common sense." This "Deweyan continuum" implies an inherent continuity between science and other cultural fields, and between academic/specialist discourse and public/lay understanding. While Dewey, then, acknowledges important differences between science and common sense,[31] he does not regard these differences as an impenetrable barrier to a commonality of knowledge among all sectors of society.

Dewey and Social Theory

More than either Peirce or James, and following Mead, Dewey understood and appreciated the social foundations of thought, believing that social meanings and effects were inherent in all forms of thought and action. His writings are threaded with commentary on the social character of problem-solving situations and the coordinated responses to them on the part of active subjects. Indeed, the challenge Dewey put to philosophy was to reject self-enclosed, abstract reflection and to engage the problems of living human beings. For him, philosophy itself, like all fields of knowledge, was thoroughly social in nature and a form of social action. As social subjects, philosophers needed to adopt a scientific outlook in the search for methodical solutions to concrete problems.

These modest observations alone provide sufficient reason to regard Dewey as an important social thinker, even without taking into account his voluminous writings on education and democracy, not to mention the widespread influence of his ideas on public life. Of particular relevance to sociologists, however, are suggestive connections between Dewey's thought and major types of social theory, including both the structural functional and interpretive action paradigms. Positioning him in the contemporary theoretical landscape runs a risk of retrospectively reading back into Dewey perspectives and ideas he might not have openly embraced. Nonetheless, as a strategy for identifying Dewey's social theoretical insights and for indicating his affinities with familiar theorists, broadly situating his work in this field can prove fruitful.

On the "determinist" side of the field, given his use of Darwinian theory, especially the notions of organism and the organic, the comparison and contrast that most readily come to mind are between Dewey and what might be called "generic structural functionalism." As is most apparent in Émile Durkheim's classic work *The Division of Labor in Society* (1965), the biological model illuminates the nature of society as a system of differentiated and interrelated parts, each performing a special function. Whereas in the structural functional model implicit in Durkheim's analysis, society is regarded as an organism and treated as an adaptive and evolving entity in a changing historical environment, Dewey's appropriation of Darwin equates "the organism" to the social actor and "the environment" to society or "the situation." But in both cases, biology supplies basic principles for conceptualizing society as a life system undergoing evolution as it adjusts to changing conditions. Dewey's notion of the social is conveyed in his frequent mention of interrelatedness and interdependence, familiar themes in structural functional logic and cardinal features of Durkheim's notion of the "organic solidarity" of modern industrial society. Far from being an argument that Dewey was a structural functionalist, these observations merely underscore the theoretical value of the biological model and the part it plays in Dewey's perception that modern society can be regarded as a system of functionally interrelated, adaptational parts.

On the "nondeterminist," or interpretive, side of the field, Dewey's ties to social theory are more apparent. A part of his work no less dependent on the Darwinian model than his overall conception of social life, Dewey's theory of experience contains numerous references to the social. The emphasis he places on subject-object relations in the form of the interaction or "trans-action" between organism and environment draws attention to the social relational character of action, in Meadian nomenclature, the interaction of self and other.[32] Against the backdrop of the rest of his work, it is clear that for Dewey adaptation is a collective effort that manifests itself in organized social activity. And Dewey sees even the isolated acts of individuals as part of a social nexus of meaning and action that constitutes the self and is the context in which thought and problem solving occurs.

Given the emphasis his theories of experience and inquiry place on active subjects, there is an obvious argument for categorizing Dewey as a social action theorist. Derived from the writings of Max Weber, "social action" has become a blanket term for theories that adopt the standpoint of the actor and are focused on interpretation and meaning.[33] However, when Dewey phrases matters in the language of social action, he attempts to strike a balance between the actor and the social environment, between "actor" and "social structure." More generally and abstractly, the defining features of Dewey's view of the dynamic relationship between subject and object are (1) an active organism functioning within a life-sustaining environment and (2) a mental apparatus that maintains an anticipatory stance toward this environment, generating adaptive behavioral responses to changing external conditions. For Dewey, society comprises social actors who function according to imagined, desired, or anticipated states of affairs in the future. This forward-looking rendering of social action is derivative of Dewey's Hegelian and Darwinian perspectives of a dynamic society undergoing evolutionary change. But it is obvious that Dewey sees change not only in terms of the impersonal, collective forces of modernity but also as guided and shaped by decision making and action on the part of social subjects. In this respect, he attempts to wed a naturalistic and evolutionary perspective to a pragmatist conception of agency.

Dewey's place in the tradition of symbolic interactionism is his most obvious and well-known connection to social theory. Largely filtered through Mead's teachings, Dewey's ideas have had a notable impact on the theorizing of Herbert Blumer and have entered into the larger constellation of sociological work drawing on Blumer's and Mead's writings.[34] The emphasis in symbolic interactionism on the meaningful and interpretive elements of behavior refracts Dewey's focus on the experiential and cognitive dimensions of action and the attention he devotes to processual concepts as opposed to structural variables. Less apparent, there is in Blumer's theory implicit recognition of the organic and coordinated character of social acts and relations, as evident in his statements about the ongoing, continuous, "back-and-forth" nature of social interaction. Blumer, however, makes an important addition to Dewey's picture of the subject-centered and creative nature of change by pointing to the *formative* effects of interaction.[35] While Dewey makes considerable use of the concept of interaction, a case could be made that his preoccupation with problem solving gives him a view of change in line with social action theory. The Meadian elements in his thought, however, suggest a strong symbolic interactionist influence (see Chapter 5). Finally, there is an interesting parallel between Dewey's translation of pragmatism into a theory of inquiry and Blumer's discussion of the methodological implications of symbolic interactionism. In both cases, a theoretical position functions as an epistemology, linking theory and method in a single framework of scientific inquiry.[36]

In a more recent development, action theory has provided important background to the sociological debate over agency and structure. Positioning Dewey as a social action theorist therefore raises questions of agency. Theories of agency commonly regard it as both creative and reproductive, incorporating the perspectives both of voluntarism and determinism, interpretation and structure.[37] The very term "agency," however, predisposes us to focus attention on the social actor and hence the dimensions of meaning and motivation. In this respect, an interpretation of Dewey's conception of agency would most closely approximate the theoretical position taken by Anthony Giddens (1979, 1984). Giddens's theory is centered on an interpretive and "meaningful" image of active, reasoning, and reflective subjects, a conception closely resembling Dewey's view of the social individual. Reflexivity plays a key role in Giddens's conception of actors, whom he sees as continually monitoring their own behavior. For him, the most important attribute of actors is their "practical consciousness," "the unarticulated beliefs and knowledge people use in orienting themselves to situations and interpreting the actions of others"

(Tucker 1998, 81). Much of this is reminiscent of Dewey, suggesting comparison to his theory of habit.[38] Giddens sees actors not as playing "roles" but as engaging in human "practices." In general, Dewey and Giddens both adhere to a view of social action that privileges cognitive factors, paralleling the approach of Meadian theory and symbolic interactionism.

Given the importance that social action and social relations held for Dewey, some final comparisons, one obvious and the other less so, can be made to Karl Marx. First, Dewey's focus on "action" has a discernible parallel to Marx's early philosophical emphasis on "practice." A second comparison between Dewey and Marx is no less significant but not as apparent. Both philosophers proved themselves highly original thinkers in perceiving the social interests shaping culture and intellectual life. With echoes of Marx's theory of ideology, the social determination of thought and knowledge is, as we've seen, an implicit and recurring theme in Dewey's work, qualifying him along with Marx as a nascent theorist of the sociology of knowledge, a dimension of Dewey's thought that reappears explicitly in Mills's early work and implicitly throughout his later writings.[39] Dewey's recounting of the history of philosophy and ideas demonstrates a perceptive grasp of the underlying social foundations, including class relations, of successive periods of cultural and intellectual development.

The social basis of thought was an idea that firmly anchored every aspect of Dewey's philosophy. Following on the foundation laid by Peirce and James, Dewey developed the central pragmatist theme of the interpenetration and consequentiality of thought and action into a comprehensive picture of society and life in general. Taking what would have otherwise remained a philosophy that subsumed the social under the logical and psychological, Dewey introduced and amplified the social dimension. While retaining a focus on the logical and psychological in his theories of inquiry and experience, Dewey's primary contribution was to shift emphasis to social relations, with a focus on social action.

This chapter has prepared the ground for a fuller treatment of the social and sociological significance of Dewey's pragmatism. Chapters 4 and 5 elaborate on what Dewey's conceptions of social action as problem solving can teach us about the practical, public, and moral meanings of sociology as a social science discipline. Through more concentrated discussion of the relationship between Dewey and the work of Mills, select aspects of their overlapping projects are interpreted as providing the constituents of a critical and publicly relevant sociology.

4

The Unity of Theory and Practice

John Dewey's polemics against Western philosophical orthodoxy can best be understood as an effort to overcome the longstanding division between theory and practice. Seeing no error in dualistic thinking more obstructive of scientific and social progress than the artificial separation of thought and action, Dewey took their unification—conceptually and in reality—as the primary goal of his effort to reconstruct philosophy along new lines. For Dewey, the pragmatist maxim first enunciated by Peirce meant that the true test of knowledge was the results it produced through action. Knowledge and theory, sustained by science and education, were authenticated in the form of practice. For Dewey, the raison d'être of thought was the intelligent guidance of human conduct toward desired ends. The union of theory and practice was thus the epistemological essence of Dewey's philosophy and the underlying principle shaping all of his work.

Dewey's comment that the experimental attitude implies "an effort to change the given" (see discussion in Chapter 3 about Dewey 1960a, 23) is an expression of his belief in the deep connection between theory and practice and a bold, liberal assertion that "practice" means changing society. The significance of this assertion for the social sciences and the role they should play in society points directly to the common ground between Dewey's philosophy and the sociology of Mills. The determination of both men to forge a link between thought and action for the purpose of progressive change is the main source of the strong intellectual connections between these thinkers.

The ambitious goal of connecting theory and practice is most apparent in Dewey's and Mills's abiding concern for bringing knowledge into the public realm. Both men were opposed to the separation of intellectual and scientific work from the problems and concerns of lay publics, and each accordingly sought ways to connect intellectual elites and professional academics with the rest of society, meaning civil society. Both Dewey and Mills were opposed to science in the service of special interests, including those of scientists themselves. Endeavoring to overcome the isolation of intellectuals, both men hoped to promote a democratization of knowledge in the belief that it is a fundamental social asset and thus a public good. Both, moreover, believed that the ultimate goal of purposive, knowledge-based social change is to enhance the rationality and well-being of the individual. For Dewey, this meant mass education and creation of the conditions necessary for growth and self-realization through life experiences that are edifying and personally fulfilling.[1] For Mills, it meant providing individuals access to intellectual resources that would enable them to understand themselves as social actors, their place in society and history, and the impersonal sources of their personal troubles. In both cases, a unity of thought and social action was the necessary condition for achieving the desired ends, which for both men was first and foremost the realization of reason and democracy.

The Legacy of Theory and Practice

Rooted in the dichotomy of subject and object, the distinction between theory and practice is a fundamental feature of Western thought. In the modern period, the differences and relationship between thought and action, knowledge and conduct, have been a recurring theme in philosophical discourse, especially in the areas of politics, morality, and ethics. Early modern thought had established a strict separation between these categories, a consequence primarily of the Cartesian dichotomization of mind and body. While in Kantian thought these concepts remained categorically separated, Hegel's dialectical philosophy depicting an interrelated, dynamic, and evolving world of ideas and culture created a conceptual landscape containing new possibilities for formulating the relationship between theory and practice. This initially bore fruit in the anti-idealist, activist leanings of the Young (Left) Hegelians, including, most notably, Marx, who grasped with powerful insight the radical social meanings and revolutionary potential of Hegel's system. Finally, an activist orientation was implicit in the antiformalist movements accompanying the rise of pragmatism (see Chapter 3), movements emphasizing the dynamic and developmental character of the modern world.

For thinkers like Immanuel Kant and Hegel, the relationship between thought and action had remained a highly formal and abstract affair. These thinkers' disembodied conceptions of theory were a reflection of the elevated status that postantiquity notions of thought had long enjoyed. Thought had always been regarded as the progenitor of action and the autonomous entity under which all human experience and activity were to be subsumed. The modern belief in progress through the systematic application of reason to human affairs served to strengthen the privileged place of thought throughout the nineteenth century. This meant prioritizing the accumulation of formal knowledge, mainly in the form of science and its troubling offspring, instrumental rationality.[2]

While recognizing the expansion of rational thought as a modern phenomenon, Dewey saw the privileging of theory over practice as the ancient root of Western philosophy itself. For him, the separation of these concepts and the prioritization of thought originated in the creation of a realm of absolute ideas detached from the "perilous" world of imperfection, uncertainty, and change.[3] In Dewey's view, the Greek preference for knowledge over action was the manifestation of a search for "immutable" and "final" principles that would give mind and soul protection against the insecurities and degradations of the real world. By promising intellectual and moral security, the fixed and universal ideas of the philosophers were from the time of antiquity highly valued by the educated classes as a shelter from the mundane and unpredictable affairs of daily life and the "lower orders." For Dewey, this "quest for certainty" among the upper social strata created a transcendental realm of ideas laying the foundation both of Western philosophy's focus on pure knowledge and a cloistering of intellectual elites (Dewey 1960b, 7–24).

In the post-Hegelian era, the privileging of thought over action was called into question by growing recognition of the action-oriented and "practical" character of modern life. According to this view, theory begets practice only to be subject to critical reformulation in light of the latter's consequences. This idea is the conceptual foundation of classic pragmatism and is most powerfully put forth in Dewey's arguments about the functional interrelations of thought and action in experimental inquiry, whereby theory is modified in response to its empirical outcomes.[4] Increasingly, as pragmatism gained ground in American philosophical circles, practice achieved equity with and increasing priority over theory. Dewey aggressively took up the challenge of questioning the autonomy of theory when insisting that philosophy achieved meaning and purpose only through engagement with the concrete problems and practices of life. This constituted a shift in emphasis toward the effects of action on theory, the cornerstone of pragmatism and other antiformalist movements that saw knowledge as enmeshed in real-life phenomena and as serving the practical interests of society as a whole. Much of twentieth-century philosophy, influenced by the empirical turn of the founding pragmatists as well as Wittgenstein, consequently took a similar position, focusing attention on practice and use as the ground of meaning and "truth."

Dewey: Thought and Action as Practice

As an antiformalist, Dewey's thinking was dominated by themes of continuity and interconnectedness. Without denying important conceptual distinctions, he insisted on incorporating into our theoretical constructions recognition of the mutual interactions of things within the phenomenal world. While his Hegelianism predisposed him to this way of thinking, the notion of interrelatedness, minus Hegel's dialectic, was ultimately concretized and given its mature form in Dewey's Darwinian model of social life. It was at this point that the couplet of theory and practice came to the fore, as Dewey began conceiving of the interconnectedness of thought and action in the context of human beings' ongoing efforts to adapt to changing life conditions.

Despite Darwin's influence, however, in treating Dewey as a philosopher of theory and practice he is first and foremost to be situated in the Hegelian tradition and the theoretical and political ideas and movements to which it gave birth. Dewey's affinities with the "philosophy of praxis" associated primarily with Marx has been widely commented on.[5] As did Marx, Dewey reacted to Hegel's idealism, its failure to engage concrete social and political realities, and its neglect of human agency. Just as Marx famously said, "The philosophers have only *interpreted* the world in different ways; the point is to change it" (from "Theses on Feuerbach," 1845, in Marx 1964, 69; italics in original), Dewey wanted to change these realities through human action. This had a rather different meaning for Dewey, of course, than for Marx. Whereas Marx sought to "transcend" philosophy by "actualizing" it through collective revolutionary action (Bernstein 1971, 54), for Dewey, changing the world meant reconstructing philosophy in a fashion that enabled it to guide enlightened action in a context of situational problem solving (ibid., 172–173). A topic of considerable controversy, Dewey's early liberal reform politics have in this regard been criticized extensively on the political Left. But while he has been held suspect and even reviled for his reformist stance, Dewey has also been praised for his active involvement in liberal and Left-leaning causes and the example he set for other public intellectuals committed to social progress.[6] Be that as it may, despite their many differences and Dewey's disavowal of revolution, Marx and Dewey shared a deep conviction in the unity of theory and practice, which both men demonstrated in their recurrent linking of knowledge to social and political action. In this respect, both thinkers held to a belief in the possibility of remaking humans by transforming society.

Dewey himself never explicitly identified his philosophy with the Marxian tradition of praxis, relying instead on the concept of "action," which Peirce in his studies of scientific logic had already made the principal focus of pragmatist philosophy. In the account of Richard Bernstein, while these terms are very close in meaning, "praxis" has retained its strong association with Marxism, while the action concept was taken up by analytic philosophers in the mid-twentieth century as a category under which to explore issues of "'intention,' 'motive,' 'purpose,' 'reasons,' and 'teleological explanation'" (1971, xvi). Certainly, as an incipient social action theorist, Dewey was concerned with these issues. Yet it hardly put him in the company of these thinkers, many of whom, though partially influenced by pragmatism, were harshly critical of him. In contrast to the concerns of the analytic philosophers, the intertwining of thought and action on which Dewey predicated his entire philosophy more closely parallels the Marxist philosophers' conception of praxis as theory manifested in the form of political action.[7]

Notable similarities between Marxist and Deweyan thought aside, "the unity of theory and practice" can be thought of in a number of ways, depending on discourse and context. In the case of Dewey, the phrase bears a rich array of interrelated meanings. This is apparent, first of all, in Dewey's understanding of concepts. In his repeated attacks on formalism, Dewey underscores the importance of avoiding static theoretical categories that detach thought from a fluid empirical reality. Such categories misrepresent the processual nature of life, which can be known only through the lens of experience. For Dewey, reality is changeful, in a state of continual flux and formation resulting from human action and ongoing changes in the environment. Our conceptual definitions, therefore, need to be given *practical* content in the broad sense of capturing the reality of these changes and the human practices shaping them. This entails developing concepts of a dynamic nature reflective of the ways that human action produces modifications in the environment through purposeful conduct.

This conception appears in several passages from *The Public and Its Problems,* first published in 1927, where Dewey addresses the question of how we approach definitions of the state. Our idea of the state, he argues, should be based on its actual manifestations, in other words, what the state looks like in practice. Dewey seems to be saying that "the state" lacks validity as an abstract, general, and fixed concept. For him, the term designates a concrete, ongoing, empirically observable entity or formation constituted by human activity. Consistent with his processual conception of social life, Dewey here is advocating the use of concepts that take a particularizing and fluid form as opposed to a generalizing and static form.

Dewey's way of thinking about "practice" as the basic principle of concept formation is evident in the following quotes. In keeping with his experimentalist inclinations, Dewey suggests that the state remains to be "discovered" through concrete effort, that its definition cannot be fixed in advance but must await the development of what "works" socially.

> Thus the problem of discovering the state is not a problem for theoretical inquirers engaged solely in surveying institutions which already exist. It is a practical problem of human beings living in association with one another. (Dewey 1954, 32)

Against the grain of traditional political philosophy, Dewey argues:

> There is no *a priori* rule which can be laid down and by which when it is followed a good state will be brought into existence. (Ibid., 33)

Finally, in a characteristically democratic and populist tone, he states:

> It is not the business of political philosophy and science to determine what the state in general *should* or must be. (Ibid., 34; italics added)[8]

Dewey proposes, in effect, that concept formation be an ongoing process, geared to actual human practices that carry us into the future, not contemplative theory or passive observation of either the past or present.[9] Concepts that are pure products of the mind fail as accounts of reality, for reality consists of the concrete actions and strivings of social actors. In this frame, the unity of theory and practice means that our concepts, definitions, and explanatory accounts, indeed our very thinking, need to be processual and provisional in character. Only by this means can they be truly representative of the evolving nature of social existence.[10]

Indeed, for Dewey the thought process itself points to the notion of practice. Thought, in his view, arises in response to a belief that something is to be done. The notion of practice is thus absolutely central to his view of the nature of thought. Dewey reminds us that theory and practice are really "two kinds of practice" (Dewey 1957, 65). Theorizing is something that people *do,* implying a set of consequences. More to the point, an idea is "a *plan of action*" (Hook 1995, 53; italics in original). Insofar as they arise in response to a need to act, ideas are by nature instrumental and situationally based, motivated and defined by a given set of circumstances. As plans, ideas imply and shape practice. In this sense, theory and practice are connected in the sense that practice *inheres* in theory.

This brings us to a second angle from which to consider how Dewey connects theory and practice. Immediately following his statement rejecting formal intellectual approaches to notions of the "good state," he presents the more conventional view consonant with modern thought since the Enlightenment. While philosophers and scientists are in no position to impose an ideal model of the state on others,

> what they may do is aid in creation of methods such that experimentation may go on less blindly, less at the mercy of accident, more intelligently. (Dewey 1954, 34)

This condenses Dewey's passionate belief in the power of intelligence and the efficacy of experimental method into a concise statement about the need to base human action on rational or, as he might say, "scientific" thought. Here, Dewey is stating the obvious, that theory precedes practice, serving as a guide to action. Despite his polemics against the idealist and intellectualist bias of traditional philosophers, Dewey's program for reconstructing philosophy thus necessarily gives equal weight to thinking *and* doing, as evidenced in the value he places on the role of education and "intelligent thought."[11]

The remainder of the quotation above draws attention, third, to the effects of action on ideas. Dewey claims that experimental method should guide action "so that men may learn from their errors and profit by their successes" (Dewey 1954, 34). Learning from one's errors is a matter of insuring that actions have theoretical consequences. Whether confirming or leading to a revision of theory, consequences are the final authority in matters of theoretical validity. For the pragmatists, a fallibilistic openness to the productive effects of error meant unrestrained testing of belief through the empirical consequences of the ideas and hypotheses emerging from those beliefs. Ideas are thus continuously subject to reappraisal depending on the outcome of the actions predicated on them.[12]

In sum, there is no shortage of explicit commentary by Dewey on the connection between thought and action. It is important to grasp, furthermore, the extent to which the connections he draws derive from his theories of experience and inquiry. First, Dewey's concept of experience abolishes the separation of the inner and outer worlds of the actor, thus integrating subject and object into a single category, a differentiated unity of thought and action.[13] Insofar as knowledge—the product of experience—is bound up with social processes, it is both source and consequence of human action. Theory for Dewey is always *about* some feature of the external world in which the subject lives and acts. Put differently, theory by its very nature implies and presupposes agency. By the same token, practice consists not of random or disconnected acts but is a more or less patterned outgrowth of theory, a manifestation and objectification of the contents of thought. Second, Dewey's account of what happens in the process of inquiry presupposes a dynamic and intimate connection between the ideas and theories guiding inquiry and their consequences in practice. The mediating link between these phases is logic, which provides the feedback loop between the outcomes of inquiry and the process of revising theory in light of its real-life effects. Thus, in the context of inquiry, theory and practice are linked by logical procedures.

The extent to which Dewey throughout his writings focuses on action cannot be overemphasized. Recognizing this, and in a worthwhile clarification of Dewey's philosophy, Mills identifies two models of action in his work. The first, derived from the natural sciences, is that of "experimentation." The second, rooted in behavioristic psychology, is the "biologistic adaptive" model (Mills 1964, 391). Mills's distinction roughly corresponds to a blurred line between Dewey's writings on inquiry and his theory of experience. These facets of Dewey's thought represent his two major and closely linked perspectives on practice, the one scientific and the other behavioral. As Mills acknowledges, these types of action are intimately linked in Dewey's understanding of the interplay of theory and practice. As Dewey sees the matter, this interplay is the dominant feature of all human endeavors and defines the dynamic character and activist orientation of modern life.

At the same time, it is important to bear in mind that the two kinds of action identified by Mills are in Dewey's view governed by the same principles of experimental method. For Dewey, *method* is not exclusive to science but integral to all human activity, including that involving moral and ethical judgments. The centrality of method is implicit in Dewey's argument that all ideas ultimately have an instrumental purpose. In short, for him the primary function of thinking is to provide the constituents of methodological procedure for a given task.[14] Intellect is always geared to the question of *how* best to do things in the interest of achieving one's goals. Dewey accordingly invokes the classic problem of means-ends relationships. Approaching thought in terms of this problem, Dewey frames theory as an activity serving a methodological purpose in the pursuit of specified ends. By defining theory and practice in terms of their instrumental functions, Dewey manages to postulate them as interrelated phases or aspects of methodological procedure, for him the foundation of not only science but also all forms of human thought and behavior.

Dewey and Mills on Social Change and Problem Solving

The foregoing discussion summarizes a number of Dewey's leading methodological precepts, many of which have long since acquired the status of basic scientific norms. The feedback loops Dewey drew between thought and action constitute the familiar relationship between theory and research that is the basis for the formation, testing, and revision of scientific hypotheses. In this respect, Dewey's better-known ideas correspond closely to common understandings of controlled scientific inquiry.

The unification of theory and practice, however, far from being a mere methodological matter, is more broadly an idea with philosophical, theoretical, and political meanings and ramifications, to which Dewey's life and work is a lasting testament. These larger meanings have significance for sociology in two respects. First, as a field that is in its broadest sense concerned with the condition and functioning of society—some might say with its "health"—sociology, as Robert Lynd (1939) argued, has an obligation beyond its scientific commitments to provide the larger society with a meaningful and comprehensive picture of itself. This would entail balancing a "passive empirical" stance that tends to reify existing social facts with an "active ideational" perspective on the role of ideas in social change and the purposive character of social action.[15] Second, a discipline in which the action frame of reference has had an important presence can benefit substantially from Dewey's theoretical insights into the nature of thought and action. Indeed, Dewey's distinctive understanding of their unity offers an original approach to social action theory.

The sociological significance of Dewey's arguments becomes apparent when viewing the unity of theory and practice in the context of two key and interrelated aspects of Dewey's philosophy: (1) an emphasis on the permanence of change and (2) his conception of human behavior as problem solving. This aspect of Dewey's thought is especially relevant to those seeking a renewal of sociological interest in social change. Relatedly, Dewey's ideas about change and problem solving offer a fresh set of conceptual terms for thinking through the agency/structure problem.

Of immediate interest, the change and problem-solving dimensions of Deweyan thought provide a frame for examining the relationship between Dewey and Mills and the Deweyan influences in Mills's work. While theoretical issues of change are less explicit in Mills's writings, the corpus of his work can be read as a study of social change, one that examines its concrete structural and historical forms and features. The strong interest Mills took in intellectuals as social change agents, furthermore, puts him in the category of an agency/structure theorist (though certainly one bereft of the abstractness of this body of theory), paralleling Dewey's belief in the role of intellectuals in bringing about progressive change. Finally, by attempting to reorient sociologists away from a preoccupation with theory and method in favor of a focus on *problems* and their connection to social structure and history, Mills imparted sociological meaning to Dewey's problem-solving perspective and his conception of society as an arena of dynamic change shaped by culture and history and guided by human action.[16]

The change and problem-solving themes pervading Dewey's thought comprise a complex of ideas that constitute the core of his social and political views. Dewey was preoccupied with the reality of change, and putting thought and action together was for him a theoretical and methodological strategy for comprehending and directing change in a rational and purposive way. In short, Dewey's philosophy, like that of Marx, is built on a metaphysics of change. It is important to realize, however, that despite his occasional historical periodizations and commentaries on contemporary societal developments, change in Dewey's writings tends to function as a generic concept. In contrast to Marxian theory, the term "change" as used by Dewey has reference primarily to the evolutionary process inherent in the ongoing interaction and mutual adaptation among social actors in relation to their environments. Dewey's concept is thus ahistorical in character to the extent that it remains abstractly lodged in the theory-practice dynamic of evolutionary adjustment. Nonetheless, Dewey's erudite writings on the evolution of culture and ideas serve to indicate the importance he attached to the social and historical contexts of change. From either angle, a sense of the inevitability and weight of change pervades Dewey's thought, shaping his entire philosophy.

Both Marx and Dewey built on the insight that thought and action are never autonomous but bound by processes of change already underway. As philosophers of theory and practice, neither thinker was able to avoid the difficulties posed by the elusiveness of social change—its ambiguities and contradictions—and the challenge of devising strategies for exercising human control over it. Both struggled with the determinism-voluntarism antinomy, Marx at the level of social and political praxis, Dewey primarily in terms of the limits and possibilities defining the complex relationships within and between the social individual and culture.[17] Marx's conception was more comprehensive, incorporating both deterministic and agentic factors while envisioning collective action in the form of organized social and political movements. By contrast, Dewey largely ignored structural and historical causation, stressing instead the notion of agency in the context of the present. While Marx mainly addressed the material, social, and political conditions effecting change in past and present societies, Dewey put primary emphasis on the *processes* of change shaping both present and future. His focus was the role of intelligence and methodical thinking in informing action that he hoped would affect the direction of change, showing little if any interest in explaining the origins, nature, and formation of such action.[18]

One gets a flavor of Dewey's thinking about the significance of change from the following quotations. In a reference to change's inevitability, Dewey comments that agency means "the redirection of changes already going on" (Dewey 1960a, 63). More to the point, in a statement powerfully joining the unity of theory and practice to social change, Dewey asserts that "intelligence develops within the sphere of action for the sake of possibilities not yet given" (65). Like experience itself, thought and action exhibit a quality of temporality. As he succinctly puts it, we "live forward" (27).

Whereas the temporal dimension is very much at the surface in Dewey's writings, it remains only implicit in Mills, despite the fact that a social change perspective is the unifying thread of his work. As we move from Dewey's philosophical categories to Mills's sociological categories, however, the question of change, important to both and a foundation of Mill's sociological practice, becomes a theme around which seeming differences between the men begin to emerge. While Dewey tended to speak in abstract generalities, remaining vague on the specific forms and dynamics of change, for Mills change meant structural and historical change involving identifiable institutions and actors.[19] The salient issues for Mills were (1) how history and the effects of social structure shape institutional and personal life and (2) how we are to identify *agents* of change that could turn society in a more enlightened and progressive direction.

Despite his appreciation of the structural and cultural barriers to change, not to mention his growing pessimism, Mills for the most part seemed to have as much faith as Dewey in the ability of science to discover and explain the causes of social ills. Also like Dewey, Mills had an enduring though somewhat faltering faith in the power of ideas to remedy such ills by means of the dissemination of knowledge through the institutions of public discourse. Also, notwithstanding his focus on the larger forces constituting society, Mills followed Dewey in keeping the individual in the picture, repeatedly returning to the human consequences of social forces. Especially in his work with Hans Gerth (1964), Mills sought to portray social science as a discipline concerned with the interface between institutions and actors, social structure and character.[20] In giving ideas a critical social role, Mills, like Dewey, posited a close relationship between theory and practice as a basis for the enlargement of freedom and reason. Mills saw this possibility as predicated on the potential of reason to initiate and direct change on the basis of sociological inquiry and the expansion of sociological knowledge within the public realm.

In apparent contrast to Dewey, however, Mills thought of the theory-practice dynamic in terms of a change strategy designed to bring about *structural transformation.* To a large degree for Mills, the success of such a strategy was contingent on an empirically based diagnosis of the constraints on and openings for change inherent in the system of power and inequality. While Dewey often only mentions power and inequality, these realities are essential aspects of Mills's analyses. Indeed, aside from *The Sociological Imagination,* the best-known parts of Mills's work consist of his "trilogy" of books on the American class hierarchy, beginning with organized labor and moving upward to the middle class and finally to the higher echelons of society.[21] On a quest to find agents of progressive change within the class structure, Mills was disillusioned by the first study, which found inroads of conservatism among labor leaders. This finding led Mills to conclude they had already been co-opted by the "system." His subsequent studies, of the power structure and the new middle class, similarly diminished his hopes for the emergence of a strong progressive politics in the United States.

Just as important, however, in keeping with Dewey's philosophical emphasis on particularity, these books exemplify Mills's enduring sociohistorical perspective and his rejection of sociology as a science whose modus operandi was generalization. Mills instead demonstrated the power of sociological investigation through his rich accounts of *particular* social and historical configurations,[22] of which his study of middle-class white-collar workers is perhaps the most notable example. This classic study in historically specific structural and cultural developments attempted to portray the social and psychological consequences of the postwar growth in bureaucracy and mass culture. With echoes of his work with Gerth, Mills was principally concerned with the characterological consequences of institutional formations appearing after the war, using sociology as a tool for examining what he perceived as the impact of these formations on the individual and society at a given point in time.

The primary disagreement between Dewey and Mills seems to arise over the meaning and implications of the notion of problem solving, the central theme of Dewey's philosophy and the ground of his reflections on action-based social change. Commentators have rightly characterized pragmatism as a problem-solving philosophy. Yet, there appears to have been scant attention paid to what problem solving actually looked like and meant to Dewey, not to mention the fit of this idea with the rest of his philosophy, including his changing political views. At once the most concrete and abstract of his ideas, problem solving based on scientific method is the reference point around which all of his propositions revolve. It is ironically both the simplest of ideas and the key presupposition of his elaborate and complex conceptual system. In Dewey's interpretation, problem solving is the core of the Darwinian dynamic of adaptation and thus serves as the axiomatic principle in Dewey's conception of change. It is in problem-solving behavior that Dewey sees the connections between thought and action to which he appeals in his call for change that is purposive and intelligently directed.

For those who believe, like Dewey, that the social sciences should be an instrument of social amelioration, the solving of problems is the unquestioned rationale for the very existence of these fields. As a theme with both scientific and moral/human meaning, the idea of problem solving reflects Dewey's deep commitment to the enlightened progress of society. Indeed, what most distinguishes his work as a philosopher and social and political thinker, giving substance to his experimentalism, is his unyielding stress on problem solving as both definitive of the human condition and the key to social progress.

At the same time, what Deweyan problem solving means for theories of agency and change has been nebulous enough to provoke critical attacks on Dewey's views. The problem-solving component of Dewey's conception of change would seem to run counter to Mills's avowed approach to sociological practice and his focus on the structural sources of human problems. Dewey tended to see problems and problem solving as situational and circumstantial, specific to time and place, and as consisting of an essentially methodological task of bringing about controlled adjustment to changing conditions. This limited, "small-scale" conception is suggestive of purposive change that is only *incremental,* in contrast to Mills's more ambitious conception of political action aimed at changing the whole system. In Mills's view, incrementalism amounted to a piecemeal approach to sociological inquiry that neglected the causal connections between the problems of milieu and larger social and historical forces.

Mills saw yet another problem with Dewey's stance on change. The experimentalist character of incremental change in Dewey meant the danger of "'implemented aimlessness,' that is, . . . futile engagement in directionless processes" (Tilman 1984, 134). Dewey refused any kind of "fixed ends" because they would "divert attention from the examination of consequences" (ibid.). For Mills, this was an unfortunate result of Dewey's experimentalist approach and an unacknowledged risk in placing one's faith exclusively in the democratic process. While Mills himself lacked an adequate theory of social change, unlike Dewey he conveyed a stronger sense of the concrete problems of existing social arrangements and the direction of change needed to realize the values of freedom and equality. Mills gave the ends-in-view of a rational and democratic society, along with a possible means of achieving them, a sociological grounding in the existing social conditions and ideologies of mid-twentieth-century America.

In short, Mills saw Dewey's approach as inadequate for addressing large-scale structural and historical phenomena. Dewey's instrumentalist model of problem solving thus appears to be incompatible with Mills's belief in the structural roots of social problems and their resolution by means of structural as opposed to situationally specific measures. However, while these contrasts might make it appear that Mills's and Dewey's positions are mutually incompatible, the logic of Dewey's ideas and his own explicit views are hardly as simple as

Mills supposed, and over time Dewey's views evolved in a way that weakens Mills's judgment of him.

Dewey and Mills on Politics: Divergence and Convergence

At the level of problem resolution and social change, the linking of theory and practice eventually raises questions of politics, as becomes evident in a contrast and comparison of Dewey's and Mills's approaches to bringing about a more democratic and rational society. The incrementalist implications of what appears to be Dewey's approach to problems open wide onto what at first glance seem like irreconcilable political differences between the thinkers. The logic of Dewey's conception of problem solving tends to align itself with the position of liberal reformism, the main target of Mills's critique of Dewey. Reiterating the familiar criticisms of political liberalism, Mills rejects Dewey's reformism on grounds of its tacit compliance with the status quo, a strategy of fixing the wrongs of the present system as a substitute for a radical critique of the entire social order. For Mills, reformism was a legitimation of existing society and inconsistent with the need for opposition to prevailing social arrangements and for overcoming the conformist elements reinforcing them in what he later called the "cultural apparatus."[23]

Along with his rejection of incrementalism, Mills more broadly took aim at Dewey's failure to acknowledge the obstacles to progressive change posed by the power structure of bureaucratic capitalism, accusing Dewey of failing to see the conflicts of interest arising from class inequalities and other inherently antagonistic social relations.[24] Mills, in effect, argued that Dewey's philosophy presupposed a harmony of social interests, whereas the property and employment relations of capitalism and its bureaucratic structures led to just the opposite. Mills and others have pointed to the contradiction between Dewey's ideal of social intelligence serving a community of common interests and a society driven by economic motives and rivalry among competing interest groups.

Ultimately, however, it seems that for Mills it was the reality of entrenched power that cast a cloud over Dewey's assertions about intelligently informed conduct within a democratic community. Mills viewed society from the standpoint of the system of power created by the modern bureaucratized economy and state. It was this system of power, in his view, with which social analysis had to contend. By not directly addressing questions of power, Mills felt, Dewey failed to recognize the severe limitations on the liberatory possibilities of thought and action and was therefore unable to theorize a workable approach to purposive change.

Certainly there is some justification for Mills's critical comments on the minimal attention Dewey paid to the structural realities of inequality and power, but in fact Mills's criticisms are highly problematic. For the purpose of weighing the merits of his criticisms, two points need to be kept in mind. First, the analytical reasoning shaping Dewey's philosophy of action and change was often at odds with his actual political views and involvements. Second, and more importantly, Dewey's politics changed over time, from an early position of liberal reformism that indeed seemed to limit political action to piecemeal efforts to a later position of socialist critique of capitalism and at least tacit support for confrontation with the power structure through collective action.

Unfortunately, Mills's reading of Dewey on change and politics is highly selective, ignoring the nuances of Dewey's thought and especially his *later* views. Mills thus presents a distorted picture of Dewey's politics, overlooking the many indications of their overlap with his own. While his claim that Dewey's reliance on the notion of biological adaptation leads to a reformist approach seems persuasive, Mills tends to read his own biases against liberalism into Dewey's conception of adaptation.[25] Although Dewey's instrumentalist tropes on adaptation and adjustment would seem to suggest a politically accommodationist position,[26] Mills tends to miss the context and actual meaning of Dewey's statements about methodical problem solving, taking them to mean only acts of adjustment to the status quo. Certainly, Dewey's statements are sufficiently general and vague as to leave room for this interpretation. One could plausibly argue, however, that Dewey's very lack of specificity creates room, at least in principle, for a variety of political approaches, including organized action directed at major social transformation.[27] In fact, upon developing sympathy for socialism in the years prior to the Depression, Dewey came around to at least passive endorsement of collective strategies for change.[28]

It is regrettable that alleged political differences should have taken on such a disproportionate significance in Mills's assessment of Dewey's philosophy. One might argue that his negative posture toward these aspects of Dewey was understandable given Mills's own faltering faith in the power of intellectual leadership to inaugurate change. Indeed, the contradiction between the potential of ideas to promote progressive action and the reality of power relations haunted Mills for much of his short life, contributing to his "disillusioned radicalism" (Geary 2009, 7–9). In his notion that public intellectuals were prospective agents of change, Mills at least concretized his belief in the unity of theory and practice, whereas Dewey's ideas remained mostly abstract and formal. To the extent that Mills's critique consisted of saying that Dewey's belief in the power of ideas over structural realities was naïve, Mills was giving frank expression to a sociologist's estimate of the uncertain structural and cultural possibilities of societal transformation. The incongruity between his own hope that intellectual activism could create the conditions of a rational and democratic society and his recognition of the empirical realities of American capitalism at least constitutes a picture more grounded than that of Dewey.

More damaging to Mills's apparent position, however, is the fact that he overlooks the many statements in Dewey's later writings referring to the structural inequalities of society as impediments to the formation of a democratic community. Sydney Hook is correct in claiming that Dewey fully appreciated the structural impediments to purposive change, seeing the "primary obstacles" as "institutional." Furthermore, hardly a naïve observer of society, Dewey saw political institutions as "concentrating power in the hands of a few" (Hook 1995, 153–154).

In a compelling account of how he sees the real meaning of liberalism in the modern age, and perhaps the most potent expression of his own views on the need for social and political transformation, Dewey's *Liberalism and Social Action* (2000), originally published in 1935, confirms much of Hook's interpretation. The chapter titled "Renascent Liberalism" contains the following passage:

> In short, liberalism must now become radical, meaning by "radical" perception of the need for thorough-going changes in the set-up of institutions and corresponding activity to bring the changes to pass. For the gulf between what the actual situation makes possible and the actual state itself is so great that it *cannot be bridged by piecemeal policies undertaken ad hoc.* (Dewey 2000, 66; italics added)

Dewey continues in this chapter to speak of the use of "force" by those in control of economic institutions and the "power" that is "exercised by concentrated and organized property interests" (ibid., 68). In this publication Dewey not only disavows "piecemeal" solutions, despite the incrementalist strategy implied by his earlier writings; he also largely refutes Mills's impression that he was blind to institutionalized power and coercion. As for the social democratic position he eventually adopted and which these passages reflect, Dewey saw socialization of the means of production as a "necessary" condition of "organized intelligence" (Hook 1995, 157). Recognizing the reality of class struggles (which he believed were pluralistic and not twofold as in Marxist doctrine), Dewey openly favored a restructuring of society along economically democratic lines.[29]

Dewey not only perceives society as divided into adversarial interest groups; according to Hook, he also "defines social problems in terms of conflicts of interest" (1995, 173). While Hook's claim on this score might be open to question, once again it is precisely the generic and philosophical character of Dewey's thinking that provides latitude for sociological and political interpretation. This raises a more fundamental objection to Mills. Even putting aside his misrepresentations of Dewey's politics, measuring a philosopher's work by the theoretical and empirical standards of the social sciences seems unwarranted, despite Dewey's considerable knowledge of these fields. Regardless, and contrary to Mills, Dewey did acknowledge the reality of social disparities and conflicts, their economic foundations, their structural character, and the need for a socialistic solution, even though he failed to seriously engage them on a sociological basis.[30]

Sociological Consequences

Despite the seeming rejection of liberal reform in Mills's criticisms of Dewey, there is arguably considerable "slippage" in the politics of both men. The evidence is suggestive of more similarities than differences between them in the realm of politics and in their overall assessment of the conditions and problems facing those seeking a more democratic society. In any case, such questions are of less importance than the common *vision* Dewey and Mills bequeathed to later generations of social scientists.

Dewey's conception of knowledge was an inseparable part of his commitment to the idea of science as a democratic and communally based enterprise. Importantly, his theoretical and methodological arguments for the connections between theory and practice established an *epistemological* foundation for this conception of science. His was a theoretical model that denied the possibility of valid and genuine knowledge except in the context of practice, which for him meant activity and action intended for a socially useful purpose. For sociologists, this implies taking up scholarly work with a social end in view and engaging in efforts to produce socially beneficial knowledge with concrete consequences. Of perhaps greater significance, Dewey's conception undermines the usually unquestioned ideal of "knowledge for its own sake." Sociological work, in his view, should be inspired and designed exclusively by considerations of its meanings and purposes for the creation of the "good society" and the enrichment of human life.

While in implicit agreement with Dewey on basic issues, Mills moved beyond his arguments, translating them into concrete sociological terms. Whereas Dewey stressed that all action was methodically based, Mills gave the question of method genuine embodiment by defining the practice of sociology as a "craft." Mills saw the sociologist as a craftsperson who relied less on codified procedures than on his or her own experiences and intellectual, social, and practical resources. Indeed, this was a very pragmatist, and pragmatic, approach to social research, giving the pragmatist experimental spirit and inclination toward methodological pluralism tangible form.[31] As Mills's most engaging and personal statement to aspiring sociologists, the essay "On Intellectual Craftsmanship" (Mills 1959, Appendix) invokes the spirit of independence and creative, nondisciplinary inquiry that was his trademark as a dedicated intellectual and down-to-earth social investigator. Even in this brief piece on research, Mills is singularly critical of "normal" sociology. At the same time, however, he is judicious in his sociological instincts, expressing a tempered skepticism toward empiricism while appealing to Dewey's insistence on the supremacy of intellect. In a statement bound to be unsettling to sociological convention, Mills says:

> There is no more purpose in empirical inquiry as such than in reading as such. The purpose of inquiry is to settle disagreements and doubts about facts, and thus to make arguments more fruitful by basing all sides more substantively. Facts discipline reason; but *reason is the advance guard in any field of learning.* (Ibid., 205; italics added)

Dewey's wide-ranging and comprehensive philosophy laid a foundation for a sociology dedicated to the resolution of social problems from within a perspective of change. Despite his recognition of the weight of culture and habit, and the encumbrances of institutionalized power, Dewey constantly emphasized the active and forward-looking character of social life and its potential for continuous betterment. While acknowledging the effects of social structure, he called attention primarily to the processual, dynamic, and evolutionary nature of society. By placing emphasis on the close relationship between practice and knowledge, Dewey shifted the focus of action theory toward cognition and learning, without minimizing the role of other factors. But of greatest importance was his repeated contention that the fundamental purpose of knowledge was the promotion of intelligently directed social progress. For Dewey, achieving this goal depended on scientists and intellectuals building strong ties between the institutions of knowledge production and public life.

By contrast, Mills's more perceptive view of society created a *tension* in his thinking between the potentiality of change inherent in knowledge and the reality of power relations and mass culture. Nonetheless, despite their differences, in his preoccupation with the social role of knowledge and its relationship to social change agents, Mills was the evident heir to the sociological and political concerns underlying and emanating from Dewey's philosophy. Notwithstanding his misplaced political antipathy toward Dewey, Mills's work represents an ambitious and passionately independent attempt to develop Dewey's vision of science in the interest of public enlightenment and the enlargement of the individual. In the spirit of Dewey's philosophy, Mills sought to create an intellectually informed and responsible sociology connected to the public realm. This was a sociology predicated on the principle that ideas and theories can serve a useful purpose only "on the ground," in the context of public discourse and democratic dialogue.

While Mills was not a social problems theorist per se, his approach to social science clearly presupposes Dewey's belief that the solving of human problems was a salient feature of social life for which all forms of human inquiry, especially science, should assume a responsibility. But whereas in Dewey the problem-solving conception of practice remains vaguely circumstantial and situational, for Mills practice meant an effort to implement large-scale structural change that would minimize or eliminate altogether the fundamental *causes* of society's problems. Accordingly, as Mills makes clear in *The Sociological Imagination* and other works, sociological analysis has a responsibility to engage subject matter that is both humanly relevant and full of substance. In this approach, the union of theory and practice is intrinsic to sociological subject matter *and* the actions of sociologists themselves. Mills stresses that scientific investigators, no less than their subjects, are social actors and therefore the bearers of shared cultural understandings of the role of knowledge in the worlds in which they act.

The imperative expressed by both Dewey and Mills to deploy the power of intellect in the interest of social progress implicitly called on specialists to become generalists, and for technicians to become intellectuals. In this view, the intellectual function of social scientists largely consists of engaging the public in rational and democratic discussion of issues and ideas. While connoting a devotion to one's chosen field of study reminiscent of Weber's notion of the "calling" (1958a), the essence of this conception is a dedication to the diffusion of knowledge within the public sphere. As we've seen, Dewey's theory of the active and "instrumental" character of ideas firmly linked the world of mind to the realm of action. This meant the extension of scientific knowledge beyond its institutionalized borders and its implementation in the wider society. The public usefulness of knowledge was thus at bottom a guiding principle for both Dewey and Mills.

Finally, the convergence of Dewey and Mills on the linking of knowledge with the public draws attention to the idea of a "public sociology" proposed by Michael Burawoy (2005b). Part of a fourfold typology of the discipline that includes "professional," "policy," and "critical" sociology, Burawoy's public sociology raises the question of how sociologists could address the public in dialogue and debate on matters of public concern. For Burawoy, public sociology is direct engagement with constituents of civil society in settings where sociological knowledge and resources are shared with nonspecialists, and the work of sociologists is informed by contacts with members of the public and their problems.

Dewey's and Mills's conception of social science clearly fits this category but represents a broader approach. Dewey's emphasis on problem solving puts him also in the category of policy sociology in which sociological knowledge is applied to the solution of social problems, while Mills's critique of the profession places him in the critical sociology category. While both thinkers promulgated the values of science and scholarship, Dewey and Mills would disavow much of the actual practice falling under the category of "professional."[32] These are only dominant tendencies, however, and beyond a point, as Burawoy correctly indicates, the four types of sociology tend in practice to overlap and draw on each other in mutually dependent and enriching ways. As Chapter 5 shows, however, while Burawoy is supportive of critical sociology, he is primarily an advocate of public sociology, whereas a discipline in emulation of the thought of Dewey and Mills would on balance seek a strong combination of Burawoy's critical and public sociologies.

As we've seen, the Deweyan and Millsian unification of theory and practice draws attention to the complicated and untidy interface between sociology and politics. These men grasped the meaning of "the political" as referring in the most general sense to any individual or collective action intended to challenge or change existing social arrangements for the purpose of creating a more democratic and rational society. More than politics in the conventional sense of contending for power or influencing people and the distribution of goods, politics for Dewey and Mills meant the much larger task of building a public sphere in which the values of freedom, reason, and democracy could flourish. Dewey envisioned this task in many ways, perhaps most famously in the form of educational practices that would cultivate the minds of young people in the ways of informed and responsible citizenship. For Mills, the goal of such a task was to develop and employ social scientific knowledge to further actors' understanding of society in relationship to their own lives.

Unfortunately, neither Dewey nor Mills was entirely successful at theorizing the extent to which a public sphere actually existed or the means by which it could be created or strengthened. At best, Dewey recognized the concentration of power as a barrier to democratic discussion and public participation, and Mills aggressively explored the consequences for civil society and character formation of a bureaucratized economy and state as well as the corrosive effects of mass culture.

In both cases, the lesson for a reformed sociology is clear. A field of study attempting to model itself on the vision of Dewey and Mills needs to investigate questions surrounding the public sphere itself.[33] This implies critical inquiry into the inroads of mass culture (consumerism, mass media, commercial entertainment) and the impact of the dominant ideologies of corporate capitalism and the state. More affirmatively, attention needs to be paid to those remaining practices and institutions (formal learning, public forums) that could nourish this sphere. In effect, the vision cultivated by Dewey and Mills reorients sociology back to its roots in civil society. This entails an active concern for protecting civil society from today's wave of neoliberal ideology that, under the rubric of "privatization," portends a colonization by the market of ever-wider segments of society.

5

Values, Social Science, Pragmatism, and Social Critique

In the words of the philosopher Hilary Putnam, "The classical pragmatists, Peirce, James, Dewey, and Mead, all held that value and normativity permeate all of experience" (2002, 30). Despite the intellectual merits of this claim, and the wide influence of these thinkers on twentieth-century thought, the conventional wisdom that factual and value judgments are incompatible and separable seems to persist. This has been true especially among social scientists, whose "value-free" proponents have attempted to portray values and valuations as "subjective" in character and therefore antithetical to the pursuit of scientific knowledge.

Concerns surrounding the impact of values have troubled social scientists ever since the time of Dewey and Max Weber, not to mention the sardonic social criticism of Thorstein Veblen. Although the value debate in sociology appears to have subsided, given its close bearing on the problem of "objectivity," the impact of values on the conduct of science remains a disputed topic. This has been the case particularly in exchanges between positivists and antipositivists, groupings with fundamentally different conceptions of both sociology's subject matter and science in general.

Despite repeated assertions that fact and value, the "is" and the "ought," belong to separate epistemological categories and therefore need to be compartmentalized, in affirmation of the view of the early pragmatists, the case for a value-free social science has been decisively refuted.[1] First of all, the separation of fact and value has long proven in practice to be a logical and empirical impossibility. In affirmation of Dewey's opposition to formal dualisms, when put to the test of experience the fact-value dichotomy loses all credibility. So thoroughly are valuations woven into our thoughts, motivations, and actions that even the futile admonition to keep fact and value separate entails an implicit value judgment.[2] As one observer puts it in reference to liberal economic theory, "The strict separation of . . . (fact and value) . . . is not, as it claims to be, morally neutral" (Streeten 1958, xliii). Value judgments are thus embedded even in putatively reasoned positions intended to defend scientific "neutrality" and "autonomy." Second, it can safely be said that attempts to maintain the fact-value separation are tantamount to suppressing the human element that is the very core of truly meaningful social analysis. Misguided efforts at segregating fact and value contradict the very nature, purpose, and distinctiveness of the social sciences.

Given the inherent ambiguity of their effects, the debate over values has been unusually convoluted. The intrusion of values has potentially negative consequences for scientific "objectivity" while at the same time promising a more substantial, meaningful, and relevant scientific practice. Valuations can be sources of bias and errors, causing unwanted misperceptions and misrepresentations of the "facts." Yet, values stand at the center of the distinctively human element that separates social from natural science and that enriches the former by combining causal explanation with meaningful interpretation. Which of these two views is to be taken more seriously is reducible in part to an epistemological and methodological issue; positivists will emphasize the objectivity problem while those more interpretively disposed will stress values' meaningful ramifications. In any case, the importance and challenge of values in social science cannot be underestimated. Values and valuations are fundamental features of all human activity, scientific and otherwise. Of crucial significance, they constitute a basic link between social science on the one hand and the larger culture of civil society and politics on the other. In this respect, the consequences of our response to the value problem reach far beyond particular disciplines into society itself.

Finally, there is a more pertinent perspective on the fact-value problem, one that is closely related to the spirit of Dewey's pragmatism. The value debate has often been a surrogate for the far more fundamental questions raised by Dewey, Lynd, Mills, and many others: What is the *purpose* of the social sciences and *whose* interests do they serve? These questions seldom get openly asked, and yet the position one takes on values ultimately depends on how these questions get answered. Such questions underlie a recurring question faced by Dewey and Mills: How can social science play a useful and critical role in the resolution of major societal problems, and what role do values play in this endeavor?

Values and the Normative Character of Social Science

It is apparent that abstract a priori reasoning presents a barrier to an understanding of the value problem, which requires grounded analysis and concrete, practical assessment of how values actually operate in the social sciences. In line with the arguments of Putnam (2002, chap. 2), instead of *dichotomizing* fact and value we need to establish a workable *distinction* between them that enables us to ascertain how they are connected and with what consequences.

An assessment of the value problem at minimum depends on consideration of the following questions: (1) How do values enter into social science? (2) Are values "subjective" or "objective," and what do these terms mean in the context of social inquiry? (3) What is the relationship of values to scientific "objectivity?" (4) How do we judge the overall import of values' presence in social science?

Crisscrossing these questions are two possible ways of approaching the problem. On the one hand, the impact of values can be considered from the standpoint of practicing theorists and researchers. Values are often thought of as primary constituents of the "subjective" outlooks and dispositions of individuals and therefore can be regarded as building blocks of a worldview or ideological position that frames the social scientist's work. On the other hand, the subject matter being investigated, involving *other* actors, is *also* inherently "subjective" in a similar sense. These are the two aspects of the perceived threat to objectivity. Not a dichotomous division, these sides of the problem are connected by mutually interactive effects that can skew research and its results in a particular direction. The valuations of the researcher influence how subject matter is selected and defined, while both facts and valuations manifested in the empirical content of research can elicit evaluative responses on the part of the researcher. In effect, the density of culture and social relations means that the researcher is in essence part of the social world he or she is investigating and therefore not a truly detached and "neutral" observer.[3]

In reality, social scientists face an amalgam of fact and value that mixes evaluative judgments with scientific method and findings. This suggests that a dichotomization of what we think of abstractly and intuitively as an axiomatic distinction turns out to be untenable in practice. The fundamental impediment to keeping facts and values separate is language itself, which frequently obscures the difference between factual and evaluative judgments. As Putnam points out, the "entanglement" of fact and value routinely manifests itself in ordinary, everyday vocabulary. Familiar terms such as "correct," "incorrect," "true," and "false," contain valuations that are embedded in the very meanings of these terms (2002, 33). By definition, we place a positive value on "correctness" and "truth" and a negative value on their opposites. More obvious is a familiar category of words such as "cruel" and "crime" that have unequivocally "normative and . . . ethical uses" (ibid., 34). Such words merge description and evaluation in a fashion that makes it virtually impossible to separate an empirical category of human behavior from its moral or ethical significance. In short, descriptive terms themselves often contain evaluative meanings, in both ordinary discourse and the specialized lexicons of the sciences and other professions.

To illustrate the latter, Gunnar Myrdal presents a short list of putatively "neutral" social science terms that are implicitly value-laden. Such words as "equilibrium," "balance," "stable," "normal," "lag," and "function," he argues, have "served as a bridge between presumably objective analysis and political prescription" (1969, 52). In actual usage, these kinds of terms imply evaluative judgments of given states of affairs, in this case in the form of subtle support for the status quo.[4]

These are common examples of an everyday phenomenon. While the language of the natural sciences and especially mathematics is another matter, the discourses of the social sciences are dependent on conventional everyday language, thereby reproducing taken-for-granted cultural meanings and valuations in what is a putatively scientific discourse. Though one implied purpose of specialist terminology is to "cleanse" social science of extrascientific influences, such efforts seldom succeed, and if anything compound the problem. The practice of what Myrdal calls "terminological escapism" (1969, 57) in effect creates a false sense of neutrality.[5]

Of the many kinds of values that could be mentioned, there are two categories that are commonly found to be most troubling, primarily because they are perceived as deep seated and highly subjective in nature. Given the ideological and partisan character of politics, the intrusion of political values is usually regarded as anathema to science. Similarly, ethical and moral values tend to be seen as covert sources of bias. An exclusive focus on such values, however, encourages a distorted picture of the involvement of science with evaluative standards. As the classical pragmatists understood, science is conducted within a thoroughly normative structure that ranges over a wide spectrum of different *kinds* of values. Putnam draws our attention to the pragmatist's insight into the inherent normativity of science when he singles out "epistemic" values, such as "coherence," "simplicity," "plausibility," "reasonableness," and the like (2002, 4, 30–31), values underpinning such familiar scientific norms as procedural rules and rules of evidence. These kinds of values are highlighted in Peirce's writings on science and Dewey's theory of intelligence (Bernstein 1999, 191–199). Such values are reflected in the normative standards governing how we define "good" scientific work, and they impart a sense of what we believe is distinctive and valuable about science and rational thought generally. For the pragmatists, especially Dewey, science was unthinkable without ethical/moral *and* epistemic values. Importantly, as we shall see below, following Dewey's conception of values, Putnam claims that both kinds of values are "objective" in nature, saying that epistemic values are "in the same boat with ethical values with respect to objectivity" (2002, 4).[6]

Weber on Values in Social Science

Before proceeding, we need to question what is meant by "subjective" and "objective" in the context of the fact-value debate and social science more generally. Some divergence can usually be found between "hard" and "soft" definitions of "subjective." In the first instance, the term refers to the distinctive emotional, idiosyncratic, or intuitive inclinations of an individual, all of which are believed to be a source of distortion or personal bias. In this sense, "the subjective" is something nonrational or irrational, the direct opposite of "the objective" (in the sense of implying "rational") and thus an obstacle to scientific thought. This way of defining the term coincides with the notion that individuals are swayed by value-related conscious and unconscious mental or feeling states that undermine scientific neutrality. While Myrdal's conception leans in this direction, by limiting himself to a discussion of valuations, which may or may not be of an emotive or intuitive kind, he tends to simply characterize all values as subjective and to equate "subjective" with "personal," leaving important questions unanswered.

By contrast, the complex and detailed arguments of Max Weber present a more comprehensive and challenging conception of the problem. While attributing more than one meaning to "subjective," Weber on balance adheres to a "soft" version of the term. Weber's remarks in "'Objectivity' in Social Science and Social Policy" (1949) locate "the subjective" in the mind but not necessarily in that of a single individual. At first, in seeming contradiction to Putnam, Weber states, "Undoubtedly, all evaluative ideas are 'subjective'" (83). But he goes on to say:

> It obviously does not follow from this that research in the cultural sciences can only have results that are "subjective" in the sense that they are valid for one person and not for others. (84)

For Weber, "subjective" is primarily a term for characterizing "culture," for him the main object of social scientific study. Accordingly, he classifies the "psychological and intellectual" (74) content of the cultural sciences as "subjective" phenomena. Indeed, Weber is noted for his interpretive methodological approach, or "Verstehende Soziologie," which takes as objects of investigation actors' subjective meanings (ideas, beliefs, values) and their motivational and behavioral correlates. By implication, in this broader conception Weber would include under "subjective" both "irrational" and "rational" factors.

While often considered less complicated, defining "objective" can be just as difficult a task as determining what is covered by the term "subjective." These definitional problems are best handled by addressing both categories at once. When Weber draws a solid line between "the sentiments" and "the analytical understanding" at the level of the researcher (1949, 60), he attempts to distinguish between "subjective" and "objective" in a way that avoids giving a clear definition of "objective" while complicating his conception of "the subjective." He does not say exactly what it is about "the analytical understanding" that is "objective." He does, however, change the meaning of "subjective," reverting here to the notion of personal bias involving emotions and ideals that presumably interfere with scientific "objectivity." In effect, for him "the subjective" has two different meanings: in one context, he applies the word to the emotional or ideological disposition of the individual (the "Vocation" lecture), in another to the "meaningful" character of culture (the "Objectivity" essay). In the first case "subjectivity" (and by implication personal valuations) hinders intellectual or scientific objectivity. In the second case subjectivity promotes objectivity. Thus, valuations are to be firmly distinguished from empirical science when they take the form of personal preferences. At the same time, valuations assuming a more "collective" form have an objective status as cultural and social phenomena and are therefore within the province of scientific study.

Perhaps of greatest importance, Weber sees values as playing an active role in the theorizing and research process.

> The very recognition of the existence of a scientific problem coincides, personally, with the possession of specifically oriented motives and values. (1949, 61)

Far from being a fact-free matter, our very judgment of what constitutes a "scientific problem" depends on a value orientation. In this sense, values serve as an instrumentality in the very selection of the problems we investigate.

Like Putnam, Weber thus appears to have an objective conception of values that he arrives at from within a sociological context by employing a technical definition of "objective." Aside from "analytical understanding," the closest Weber comes to defining "objective" is his reference to "an unconditionally valid type of knowledge in the social sciences, i.e., the analytical ordering of empirical reality" (1949, 63). In subsequent discussion, however, he further complicates matters by stating, "There is no absolutely 'objective' scientific analysis of culture" (72). With the exception of his injunction to keep "sentiments" out of "analysis," Weber seems to see no possibility of maintaining a separation of facts and values in the practice of what he calls "cultural science." This view informs his historicist methodological approach, whereby the object of study is conceptualized as a distinctive social and historical configuration or "historical individual" (79). Such an entity gets identified and defined solely on the basis of its cultural and historical "significance" *in terms of* a given "value orientation." Judgments of facts are thereby seen as derivative of judgments of an evaluative nature.

Paralleling the emphasis Dewey put on "the particular" and Mills's historicizing of social structure, Weber the historicist disavows the search for immutable laws of causation, claiming validity for only empirically identifiable, particular, delimited patterns of sociocultural meaning. Such patterns can include historically specific relations of causation but are unlike causal explanations of the kind involving general laws, common to the natural sciences (1949, 75–81). Rather,

Weber's particularistic conception sees causation as involving singular patterns of ideas and motivations.

As if to leave no doubt of his conviction that social science is of a particularizing as opposed to generalizing character, as well as his acceptance of the subjective/cultural limitations of investigators, Weber asserts that "all knowledge of cultural reality . . . is always knowledge from *particular points of view*" (1949, 81; italics in original). "Objectivity" for him ultimately seems to mean employing the most effective method of representing what is only a piece of reality in a fashion that *recognizes* it as no more than a partial yet meaningful picture. Weber's reflections converge on two general strategies for accomplishing this. One is to *acknowledge* the value-determined interests shaping social/cultural/historical analysis and one's choice of problems. The second strategy is to develop an *approximate representation* of an "historical individual" by means of an "ideal type" concept, a special analytical construct that, based on a "one-sided accentuation" (90) of a singular viewpoint, seeks to identify both common and distinctive features of a given historical pattern.[7]

Weber's intricate analysis demonstrates that values are to be thought of in different ways at different levels and stages of the investigative process. Far from positing an unbridgeable gap between facts and values—a common but badly mistaken interpretation of his position—Weber's propositions establish a close interconnection between the two categories.

Insofar as the fact-value distinction is seen as an issue of "objectivity," we can draw the following conclusions. Keeping valuations out of sociology is unattainable, but taking them seriously as a core part of the field is imperative for a science worthy of its name. "Scientific objectivity" depends not on efforts to rid the field of valuations but rather on strategies for bringing them to conscious awareness and making them a manifest and integral part of theory and research. As Weber and others have argued, this is not only an essential condition for accuracy in social inquiry; it is also the closest we can come to a meaningful definition of "objectivity." Myrdal (1969, 55–56) essentially concurs when he states that making one's own value preferences explicit is a first step in controlling for hidden bias while imparting genuine meaning to the subject matter. Finally, consonant with Weber's statement that sociologists study *problems,* Mills declared, "No problem can be formulated unless the values involved and the apparent threat to them are stated" (1961, 129).[8]

Many concede, perhaps reluctantly, that values and valuations are an unavoidable feature of the scientific process but continue to define the situation as presenting a procedural or methodological problem of controlling for "extrascientific" factors. Others, agreeing with Weber, accept values and valuations as vital and decisive factors in the pursuit of knowledge and essential components of sociological explanation. Yet others, adopting Mills's position, see social science as based on valuations and as appropriately and overtly conducting itself on their behalf. Indeed, Mills's approach presupposes the pragmatist refusal to partition fact and value, a position at the core of Dewey's writings and a further obvious influence of Dewey and Weber on Mills's sociology.[9]

It is noteworthy that Weber's conception of social science as structured by values and based on a methodological protocol emphasizing particularity converges both with Dewey's abiding concern for values and his historicist perspective.[10] Similarly, the Weberian conception reappears both in Mills's belief that values shape the subject matter and practices of sociology and in his focus on historical social structures. Most important, the intellectual and theoretical affinities among these theorists and their arguments in support of the centrality of values offer solid ground for Putnam's appeal to an objective conception of valuation. In Dewey's case, this conception originates in his strong concern for morality and its relationship to science as well as his interest in developing a scientific theory of ethics.

Dewey on Values, Science, Morality

American pragmatism and social science were born in an atmosphere of waning Victorian values and an emerging secular culture shaped by the growing authority of science and a growth in commercialism and the market economy. With religion in relative decline, Dewey feared these trends would undermine morality and a sense of community and common purpose essential to a truly ethical and democratic society.[11] While embracing the scientific method, Dewey was disturbed by the strain placed on time-honored beliefs and values by the discoveries of natural science. As a consequence, he regarded a reconciliation of the two domains a pressing challenge, asking bluntly, "How is science to be accepted and yet the realm of values to be conserved?" (1960b, 41). In effect, Dewey rendered the problem of "the traditional" versus "the modern" as a challenge of creating compatibility between scientific knowledge on the one hand and values essential to the well-being and progress of society and its members on the other.[12] This meant reconstructing values along secular and scientific lines together with the creation of scientific goals and practices that would meet the moral needs of society (Bernstein 1999, 218).

Dewey at times characterized the transition from religion to science as involving a loss of the *human* dimension of life. The scientific study of nature revealed a reality beyond the realm of human values and was therefore indifferent or blind to the moral, spiritual, and other needs of the individual. The shift from a human-centered world to one based on the impersonal, immutable laws of nature thus entailed, in Dewey's view, a kind of dehumanization that threatened personal beliefs and a trust in the efficacy of human agency. Equating, in Durkheimian style, "the moral" and the "social,"[13] Dewey correspondingly underscored the inseparability of "values" and "the human." Overall, he saw adaptation to modernity as chiefly a problem of sustaining and reconstituting the realm of values in a manner conducive to social progress and, ultimately (and by Darwinian implication), survival. Hence, Dewey's philosophy was preoccupied with questions concerning the task of integrating values with the project of modern science in a fashion that was mutually accommodating, reconstructive, and beneficial to both.[14]

Dewey saw this not as a matter of connecting two different spheres, although the separation of science from the rest of society was a historical process already underway. Rather, he argued that science was *predicated* on values and that values in the modern world in turn depended on scientific inquiry; the two spheres were internally related and mutually dependent, thus forming a unity. More broadly, the social relations of science made it a moral enterprise, connecting it to the larger society and the general interest. As Rick Tilman puts it, "Dewey believed that scholarly work was inherently social and that this fact implied a deep moral obligation" (1984, 131).

Dewey's conception of morality was extraordinarily broad and elastic. While "values" meant primarily *moral* values, referring to questions of "right" and "wrong," he didn't always draw a clear distinction between the cognitive/rational and moral/ethical conceptions of these terms, perhaps because he regarded them as representing two sides of the same coin. In Dewey's hands, these words had nuanced and fluid meanings that shifted with context and situation. At times, "moral values" referred to a particular kind or category of values, those directly pertaining to how one should or should not act as a member of a group or society.[15] At other times, Dewey, following Peirce, regarded values per se as having a moral character and thereby carrying moral force insofar as they defined what were deemed "correct" and "incorrect" choices and ways of doing things *in general.* Values, in other words, were in some sense *generically* moral in character.

Contrary to what might appear to be the case, Dewey's conception of the connection between science and morality is not "tacked on" to his experimentalist philosophy but inheres in fundamental pragmatist principles. First and foremost, pragmatism posits the consequences of ideas and actions as the basic criteria for judging their worth. Being largely a matter of the outcome, or effects, of our thoughts and actions, a notion of morality is thus implicit in the pragmatic maxim discussed in Chapter 3. A more obvious manifestation of Dewey's preoccupation with morality is the problem-solving orientation of his philosophy. Moral convictions and commitments form part of our motivation to solve problems as well as providing evaluative standards and tools for doing so, furnishing scientific and practical procedures with moral guidelines. The very notion of problem solving, by which Dewey ultimately meant the solving of social and human problems, carries moral connotations imparting to science a sense of moral purpose as an instrument for improving the human condition. In short, the theme of problem solving per se, conceptually and practically, connects science to morality.

The counterpart of Dewey's interest in the moralization of science was his wish to construct a methodical approach to morality and eventually a scientific theory of ethics.[16] Recognizing that the absolutisms of religion, tradition, and custom were impediments to experimental and pluralistic forms of thought and inquiry, Dewey sought a means of putting questions of morality and ethics on an empirical and practical basis. As a prelude to an ethical theory, Dewey in many of his texts presented the rudiments of a theory of values and valuation, the main outline of which can be found in his *Theory of Valuation,* first published in 1939 (1966b). Elaborating on the difference between what is "desired" and what is "desirable," Dewey, in his customary antidualistic mode, disposes of "subjectivist" theories, which locate value in personal desire, and "objectivist" theories, which locate value in the desired objects (Brinkmann 2013, 112). Transcending this dichotomy, he argues that our conception of the desirable is a product of thoughtful deliberation, involving intelligent judgment regarding what is "good" in a general or universal sense. The desirable, in short, is a concept rooted in thought and intrinsic to the relationship between thought and action.

By means of this reasoning, Dewey contextualizes values in the unity of theory and practice, locating valuation behaviorally in "the act"—in social relations, actions, and interactions—as opposed to either personal preference or the qualities of objects themselves. Dewey thereby sees an objectification of values emerging from the deliberative mental and social processes involved in a determination of "desirability" as something separate from both individual desires and the characteristics of objects. Dewey's conception of values thus places them in the category of what Durkheim called "social facts," in the sense of being collective products arising from associational life. For Dewey, however, as fruits of thoughtful deliberation, values are not merely by-products or artifacts of group experience but ideals to be pursued and intelligently cultivated for the good of society.

Dewey, in agreement with Weber, further considers values as objects of empirical study, saying:

> Since desire and interest are behavioral phenomena (involving at the very least a "motor" aspect), the valuations they produce are capable of being investigated as to *their* respective conditions and results. Valuations are empirically observable patterns of behavior and may be studied as such. (1966b, 51; italics in original)

Putnam stands in agreement with both Weber and Dewey that values, whether in the form of subjective preferences, the qualities of objects, or collective notions of the desirable or general good, are just as subject to empirical investigation as any other observable phenomenon. As he puts it, "What is valid for inquiry in general is valid for value inquiry in particular" (Putnam 2002, 110). Putnam, furthermore, in line with Dewey's view of "the desirable," underscores that the objective status of values in this sense means they are also subject to our powers of rationality. As he argues, "It is time we stopped equating *objectivity* with *description,*" saying, "There are many sorts of statements . . . that are not descriptions but are under rational control, governed by standards appropriate to their particular functions and contexts" (ibid., 33; italics in original). In other words, though values may not always be "describable" in the familiar sense of the term, values and valuations not only are real facts amenable to scientific discourse but also, as Dewey implied, exist within the province of reasonableness and rational judgment.[17]

The Concept of Critique

By demonstrating the indispensability of values to scientific work, Weber, Dewey, Mills, and Putnam established a basis for the idea of a critical sociology based on normative criteria. Not only do values imply deliberative judgment and choice among competing alternatives; evaluative judgments are inherently critical insofar as they question empirical reality as well as one's own interests and motivations. In the presence of values, reality and its analysis do not speak for themselves (as in positivist sociology) but are subjected to normative challenges. Values, therefore, are the substratum of critical approaches to social inquiry.

While none of these thinkers outlined a program for the development of a critical sociology, by virtue of the close connections they established between valuations, theory, and science they disclosed the *implicit critical potential* of classical social theory, a body of work rooted in Enlightenment and normative ideas of reason and democracy. More to the point, in their efforts to reconcile science and values, Weber, Dewey, Mills, and Putnam taken together offer constituents of a critical sociology explicitly predicated on valuations. Notwithstanding possible objections to the inclusion of Weber in a grouping of pragmatists, this raises the possibility of an innovative pragmatist-based sociological approach to social critique.

A modern idea with multiple meanings and uses, the notion of critique is traceable to nineteenth-century philosophical, social, and political thought. It is also today a common notion in literary and artistic criticism. Generally speaking, critique is a process of engaging in critical questioning and systematic analysis of a given object or state of affairs for the purpose of evaluative assessment. In its generic meaning, critique involves both positive and negative judgments intended to reach a comprehensive evaluation. In social and political theory, however, the dominant tendency in critique has been toward negative or oppositional arguments formulated within a normative and sociohistorical framework. This type of critique preoccupies itself with normative standards themselves, specifically their "fit" with a given set of empirical conditions. The structure of this type of critique generally is both analytic and synthetic, concerned with understanding the "whole" and its relationship to the "parts." Accordingly, this type of critique rejects closed theoretical systems and formal schema, presupposing instead the historical, changeful, and contingent character of knowledge and "truth," the underlying premise of most modern philosophy since Hegel and Darwin and a major precept of Deweyan thought. Thus, critique always operates within a historical framework that is the context for empirical and evaluative statements and arguments.

The work of the postwar critics presented in Chapter 2 approximates select aspects of this sense of critique by engaging in critical descriptive accounts of American society at a given point in time. As illustrated in the case of Mills especially, social critique often employs sociological ideas and methods and, (in accordance with Weber) like all sociological analysis, makes an appeal to value orientations in the determination of what constitutes a societal problem. Like literary criticism, social critique examines constituent elements of its object of study (institutions, social practices), analyzing and interpreting them contextually as a means of developing an assessment of the whole work (society as a whole). As Mills demonstrated, this entails examining major components of social structure and culture, overarching social ideas and ideologies, and the dynamics of change shaping both present society and its future tendencies. This is exemplified by Mills's practice of relating parts to the whole within a historical context while employing a mode of inquiry in which normative criteria become a means of assessing the *human* features and meanings of social structures and arrangements.

In a predominantly negative posture, social critique presupposes that something is fundamentally defective or dysfunctional with society. The postwar critics viewed American society as failing in a variety of ways to adequately fulfill the genuine needs, ideals, and aspirations of upwardly mobile individuals. Bringing normative considerations to bear, these critics drew on sociological and journalistic methods to characterize these failings in terms of changing attitudes, values, and character structure. Though weak in substantive theory and causal explanation, this body of work illustrated how values form a vital part of this kind of criticism, a point of view taken for granted by Mills in particular.[18] Mills's own work presupposed a need to preserve the values of freedom and reason, values he considered "the thread of classic social analysis" (1961, 130) and that he saw as threatened by bureaucratization, power structures, and the deceits of mass culture. Other critics, too, articulated the values behind their critiques of society. Predating the postwar critics, Veblen referred to an "instinct of workmanship," which provided a normative ground for his critique of the degradation of pride in work in a privately owned system of machine production. He saw this "instinct" further violated in the rise of conspicuous consumption as a compensatory means of accumulating social esteem in the absence of productive achievement (1934, 16, 93). For Riesman, who was critical of the social adjustment ethic of the other-directed personality, a fourth character type expressing the value of "autonomy" became a normative criterion for his consideration of historical personality types (1960, pt. 3).

Consistent with Weber's conception of sociology as a cultural science and Lynd's argument for integrating the social sciences around a focus on the whole culture, these critics believed that social phenomena had meaning only within a framework of cultural values. Indeed, most of the works in this genre could be regarded as *studies* in values, insofar as they explored the attitudinal and behavioral effects of social change in terms of shifts in value orientations. These studies took values as a frame of reference in attempting to define the type of person characterizing a particular historical social structure. In doing so they also provided concrete illustrations of how cultural values link person and society.[19]

What perhaps today most distinguishes the postwar critics' version of social critique was their ability to employ a type of analysis and discourse accessible to the tastes and needs of an educated reading public. They accomplished this largely by avoiding the formal esoterica of "impartial" studies that in the name of "objectivity" were designed to *eliminate* the human factor. As against this, these writers made the human factor the *focal point* of analysis, bringing humans back in. They did this in a manner both relevant and available to thoughtful and concerned readers. In this respect, these critics were unique in making public discourse and understanding a crucial feature of critical social inquiry.

Immanent Critique

The main shortcoming of postwar social criticism, with the partial exception of Mills, was its lack of a normative framework that enabled methodical criticism from within a comprehensive theoretical and epistemological position. The best-known model of such a framework is the Hegelian-Marxist tradition of immanent critique associated with the Frankfurt School of critical theory.[20] Immanent critique is a distinctive *method* of social critique that goes beyond the Millsian approach by critically examining society in terms of its "self-understandings." This type of critique proceeds from the standpoint of society's own avowed ideals, with the aim of disclosing contradictions between "the ideal" and "the real" as manifested in prevailing social practices. Such contradictions are seen as engendered by the dominant social powers in the pursuit of their own interests.

An approach developed by Marx in his analyses of the structural and ideological contradictions of capitalism, immanent critique was used by members of the Frankfurt School in explorations of what they perceived as new forms of social domination in advanced capitalist society. In a revision of Marx, Frankfurt thinkers saw the structures of capitalist modernity precipitating a crisis in the ideals of reason and freedom in the form of "instrumental rationality," a Weberian concept given famous expression in the term "iron cage."[21] Seeing the contradictions of twentieth-century capitalism in terms of a crisis of *subjectivity,* the Frankfurt School believed that consciousness was now being penetrated by increasingly subtle, complex, and powerful forms of ideology. This development manifested itself most directly in the form of a "culture industry" that cloaked the system's internal contradictions and manipulated social consciousness to conform with the interests of the dominant powers, thereby forestalling or dispelling opposition to existing arrangements.

Immanent critique thus attempts to reveal how the ideological processes of society effectively mask contradictions between purportedly consensual ideas and beliefs—how society "sees itself"—and its concrete reality. Examples abound in American society of, for instance, the contradictions between the ideal of equality and its superficial appearances and the reality of inequality, between the American Dream of prosperity and the reality of widespread poverty, and between proclamations of support for Enlightenment values of reason and democracy and the irrational consequences of capitalist society with its rule by powerful economic and political elites.

Immanent critique finds the source of societal problems and potential instability in the structural and cultural contradictions of the whole society. Those immanent critiques retaining overtones of Marxism go even further, and against Frankfurt thinkers, to envision system breakdown as creating dynamic forces of emancipatory change in the form of social movements and revolt against the system.

Despite its particular political, moral, and theoretical origins and intent, the analytical method of immanent critique can serve as a model for social critique generally. For purposes of social inquiry, the method can be appropriated in its basic outline, retaining its normative character and moral/ethical purpose, without necessarily reproducing its Marxist themes. This method is highly adaptable to critical sociological analysis, as has been demonstrated in numerous normatively oriented studies of social problems and social change in which principles of immanent critique are implicitly or explicitly employed. At the same time, few would argue that it is possible to practice immanent critique without encountering numerous problematic conditions traceable to the system of capitalism. Given its analytical depth, when applied at the level of the whole society, this kind of critique invariably exposes characteristics of capitalism that explain its continued dominance and predictable social deformations.

Social Critique as Diagnosis

The connections between immanent critique and critical strains in the classical sociological tradition, primarily the work of Marx and Weber, are suggestive of a number of genealogical and theoretical continuities between critical and social theory. Both lines of development emerged within what Hans Sluga (2014) has called "the diagnostic turn" in philosophy and political thought during the nineteenth century.[22] The diagnostic approach rejects the abstract speculative mode of traditional philosophy, adopting instead a critical and historically based stance toward the crises of modernity and its concrete problems, seen within a framework of the unity of theory and practice (ibid., 25). The unmistakably Deweyan flavor of this description situates him, too, in the diagnostic tradition and is yet another indication of Dewey's affinity with the Marxist tradition of critical social theory.

The basic commonality between immanent and other types of social critique can thus be seen in their diagnostic character. Most conventional sociological work tends to restrict itself only to the *symptoms* of social dysfunction. By contrast, social critique, like much of classical social theory, is in search of what lies *behind* these symptoms in the overall logic, structure, and condition of society. In its essential form, critique emulates the medical model of diagnosis, which identifies problems of the human body by interpreting bodily symptoms. These symptoms are read as signs of abnormality, indications that something is wrong with the patient that requires remedial treatment. Following a determination of the underlying *causes* of the symptoms, corrective action is taken in an effort to eliminate these causes, thereby returning the body to a healthy or "normal" state. In sociology, poverty and crime, for example, can be read as symptomatic of socioeconomic dysfunction or abnormality in the "social body." The causal explanation provided by immanent critique might be the contradiction between the "land of opportunity" ideology and class-related structural and cultural barriers to upward mobility. Whether or not employing the principle of contradiction, sociologists practicing critique are thus in effect acting as "social diagnosticians" insofar as they are engaged in critical assessment and causal accounting of social ills.

A classic model for this, its incongruities with critical theory notwithstanding, is Durkheim's study in which suicide (and by extension crime, violence, and other social pathologies) is interpreted as a sign of an abnormal social condition, for the French sociologist a state of anomie, or "normlessness."[23] While Durkheim's ideas might seem only tangentially related to the diagnostic tradition discussed by Sluga, his theory of anomie follows the diagnostic model of thinking by singling out a behavior pattern that he attempts to explain in terms of underlying social and cultural conditions.

In sharp contrast to the functionalist outlook of Durkheim, however, social critique in the mode of immanent critique and critical theory examines the deep systemic *sources* of social and human dysfunction, indicating how eliminating its causes depends on changes in the *system itself.* In this context, system dysfunction is defined in terms of its failure to fulfill basic *human* needs, not the system needs implicit in Durkheim's conception of normative breakdown. This mode of inquiry and evaluative analysis is exemplified by the Marxist critique of the prevalence of alienation and poverty in early industrial capitalism, a critique predicated on beliefs in the intrinsic value of the individual and basic democratic principles.[24] Derivatively, in the American context, the central contradiction defining system dysfunction in human terms is that between the ideologies and realities of capitalism on the one hand and the ideals and goals of democracy and the fulfillment of basic human needs on the other.

In addition to its use in identifying disjunctions between ideals and reality, the concept of contradiction can be applied sociologically at a nonideological level.[25] This use of the concept consists of a theory and method for assessing the *structural* contradictions of society. This has taken different forms, but Marx's analysis of the contradiction between the institution of private property and growth in the social means of production remains a pertinent example. Marx saw this as the central contradiction of nineteenth-century capitalism, the primary source of the alienation and oppression of the industrial working class, and the pressure point of system breakdown and revolutionary change. A comparable example of structural contradiction exists today between the existence of a domestic American job market established on the basis of manufacturing and services and the rapid growth of informational technologies driving globalization. This historical process is creating globalized patterns of employment that shift American jobs overseas while these selfsame technologies facilitate the concentration of wealth in the high-tech world of international finance.[26]

The foregoing illustrates two possible uses of the notion of contradiction. In one case it involves *ideological* analysis, and in the other, explanations of the *structural* sources of social problems, most notably economic and social inequality. At the same time, the Marxist version of structural contradiction (forces of production versus relations of production) is not entirely applicable to the more developed and complex structures of contemporary society, and despite its explanatory power, the idea of contradiction itself is not definitive of either social critique or critical theory. Both bodies of work are sufficiently comprehensive in scope and purpose to draw on ideas and methods from a variety of theoretical perspectives, including that of pragmatism.

Pragmatism and Social Critique: Critical Dimensions of Dewey's Philosophy

We find in classical pragmatism, specifically in the writings of Dewey, recurring references to the notion of a radical democratic community. From the beginning, pragmatism displayed a democratic style of thought, apparent in Peirce's vision of a community of scientists, implied in James's celebration of human experience, and evident in Dewey's enduring belief that reason was possible only under genuinely democratic conditions. Dewey took democracy and reason seriously as inseparable twins of the Enlightenment, a tempered version of which informed many of his views. The Enlightenment ethos of progress was a particularly strong influence on Dewey, reinforcing his faith in science and the virtues of social and political action.

While animated by Enlightenment ideals, however, Dewey rejected the absolutisms accompanying this philosophy and embraced instead the dynamic and evolutionary viewpoints of Hegel and Darwin, the main sources of his conception of a pluralistic, dynamic, and continually evolving social universe. These aspects of Dewey's philosophy contributed to his critical perspective by orienting him to the potentialities of human intelligence and action in an indeterminate and unfinished world. Reminiscent of Marx, Dewey effectively brought Enlightenment ideals and Hegelian categories down to earth in the particulars of historical, social, and political reality and the needs and possibilities they presented for change.

In doing so, however, Dewey's project departed from orthodox Marxism and its animating teleology focused on the revolutionary overthrow of capitalism. Largely dispensing with notions of contradiction and the conflict model of two opposing classes, Dewey saw multiple forces at work in a society that he described in evolutionary, pluralistic, and sociocultural terms. For Dewey, democracy was not dependent on a transformation of the "economic base." Rather, democracy could and even needed to be realized within existing property relations by means of institutional changes—transformation of the "superstructure"—that would promote more egalitarian and participatory forms of association. In this respect, Dewey diverges sharply from Marx's scenario of class revolution by embracing a radical democratic politics that envisions strategies for *ameliorating* the harsh and unjust effects of a market-based, privately owned economy. Despite their philosophical affinities, then, Marx and Dewey followed different theoretical and political paths to the formation of a democratic community: for Marx it should be a community of "producers" attained by revolution and for Dewey a community of "social actors" achieved through institutional reform.

Dewey's non-Marxist trajectory can be understood in terms of his intellectual commitment to basic pragmatist principles and their compatibility with American culture and experience. Indeed, his exceptionally comprehensive work was largely an outgrowth of his ability to adapt Hegelian and Darwinian ideas to the American context. Dewey found the fundaments of pragmatism as much in the American proclivities for the social-psychological, practical, and experimental as in the critical and historical methods of the Hegelian tradition, a combination that gave his philosophy an unusual power.

Dewey's accomplishments in this regard are all the more remarkable given the differences between European and American philosophy and social thought. Scholars steeped in European intellectual traditions, especially German philosophy, have typically looked upon pragmatism with disfavor if not contempt, regarding it as an expression of an American disposition toward narrow technocratic and utilitarian thinking.[27] This faulty charge is among many that Dewey's work still endures, largely based on misunderstandings he engendered by failing to sufficiently clarify certain of his ideas, especially the meaning of the term "instrumentalism." Fortunately, continental prejudices against pragmatism have diminished in the wake of the work of second-generation Frankfurt theorist Jürgen Habermas, whose highly respected writings incorporate into critical theory ideas from Peirce, Dewey, and Mead. Habermas has attempted to strengthen critical theory through an assimilation of notions of a free and democratic community based on principles of unconstrained social interaction and symbolic communication (Antonio 1989; Antonio and Kellner 1992; Jay 2016, chaps. 6 and 7). Appropriating a range of ideas from Anglo-American theories of language and communication, Habermas subsumes much of this material under the Meadian concept of symbolic interaction, which he claims offers an emancipatory model of speech and communication. In a summary of Habermas's thinking, Robert Antonio states, "The core idea is that a universal ideal of *uncoerced communication* underlies symbolic interaction" (1989, 732).

Despite the multiple influences shaping Habermas's assessment of pragmatism's critical potentials, an exclusive focus on Dewey and Mead suffices to indicate the gaps in classical critical theory that Habermas addresses and how they can be overcome by pragmatist ideas, ideas with deep ties to Hegelian-Marxist philosophy. Based on his early exposure to Hegel, Dewey established certain habits of thought paralleling those of the Marxist tradition of critical social analysis, as indicated by Dewey's humanist orientation, historicist outlook, antipositivism, and critical responses to the deleterious effects of capitalism. Despite these tendencies, Dewey, as we have seen, was not a Marxist nor did he seem to find any use for the dialectical method with which the idea of contradiction is often associated. Nor was "emancipation" or the terminology of immanent critique part of his vocabulary.

Still, by declaring that philosophy had a social and moral purpose, Dewey defined this field as an evaluative enterprise engaged with the real problems of human society and possessed of the logical and scientific tools for critically appraising them.[28] In his attack on dualisms, Dewey successfully fought against the split between the intellect and material existence, reuniting theory and practice and thereby reconnecting reason to experience (Kadlec 2006, 530–533). Change and growth, innate to life itself, were seen by Dewey as embodying the conditions of possibility for social and moral progress, developments for which the experimental attitude and method were necessary preconditions. Toward this end, the pragmatist commitment to the idea of a community-based radical democracy informed by social and scientific knowledge meant that society was to be the object of sustained criticism and ongoing experimentation.

The social-theoretical view informing this conception redresses elements of Frankfurt School thought that have been the object of considerable criticism, most notably its one-dimensional perspective and essentially pessimistic and passive outlook on what Herbert Marcuse and other members of the school referred to as "the totally administered society" (1964). As critics have argued, it was largely the Frankfurt School's adherence to a "philosophy of consciousness," which locates reason within the isolated, contemplative individual, that was a prime source of its inability to develop a convincing theory of domination and, importantly, emancipation.[29]

From a pragmatist perspective, this shortcoming, partly an outcome of the school's Freudian tendencies, stems from a failure to recognize thought as a *social process*, as theorized in Mead's writings and as appropriated in Dewey's conception of reason as an outcome and embodiment of social relations and practical experience. In Mead's theory, "taking the role of the other" (1956, chap. 7) involves a sharing and exchange of attitudes, implying a "rich intersubjectivity" (Antonio 1989, 738) that contextualizes reason in social interaction. While assuming a condition of rationality, Mead's concept, expressed as "the generalized other," breaks with the exclusively rational presuppositions of classical critical theory by including, in Antonio's words, "the capacity for sympathetic identification with other persons' needs, sufferings, and feelings" (ibid.). The Meadian strains in Dewey's thought thus provide critical theory a crucial social-psychological perspective on the human dimensions of associational life. This shifts social critique from a restrictive focus on the conservative tendencies of social structural and cultural constraints to the potentials for change inherent in the symbolic processes and social dynamics of group life, factors generative of human agency and action.

The Meadian ideas in Dewey have several specific consequences for a concept of critique. First of all, Meadian theory locates the origins of normative criteria in social relations, not abstract reflection, on which Frankfurt critical theory heavily depended. Second, Meadian social psychology projects a democratic conception of society. The democratic narrative running through Dewey and Mead accordingly affords many of the components of normative thinking on which social critique depends. This feature of pragmatism, furthermore, refracts a democratic conception of reason and knowledge as opposed to the "elitist" conception often attributed to the Frankfurt School.

A further productive difference lies in Dewey's confidence in science, a noticeable contrast to the predominantly gloomy Frankfurt view, which tended to reduce modern science to positivism in all of its ideological ramifications. While clearly recognizing the conservative implications of positivism, Dewey, as we have seen (in Chapter 3), held to a more nuanced position, refusing positivist science on predominantly epistemological grounds while seemingly leaving room for a limited use of positivist methods. He held to a practical understanding of science as a pluralistic, democratically based, and experimental method of knowledge production, for him a method essential to all purposive human activity. Dewey would see his experimentalist approach, furthermore, as implying a need to engage in normative critique of the very values and criteria informing the *practice* of critique, a neglected task of classical critical theory. This self-reflexive approach is an analogue to Mead's observation that we can make objects of ourselves, implying a capacity for self-criticism. This approach is an expression also of the Meadian conception of behavior as governed by a symbolic process of recognition, interpretation, and potential reworking of socially shared norms. On all counts, Dewey's understanding of modern science was more open and expansive than that of the Frankfurt School.

Of considerably more significance than the action frame of reference tying him to Weber, the symbolic interactionist elements in Dewey's pragmatism geared his thinking to the liberating potentials of human interaction. This body of theory builds on ideas about the creative role of agency in social change and the power of symbolization to facilitate change in consciousness. As such, Dewey's pragmatism brings not only balance to the overly deterministic outlook of Frankfurt School theory but also a framework of critique amenable to sociological theory and inquiry. In this respect, his work, and pragmatism as a whole, represents, at least prefiguratively, a philosophical and theoretical approach in keeping with the tradition of critical theory.[30]

Reprise

Questions regarding the validity and function of normative criteria in the practice of critique, finally, bring us back to the problem of values. This chapter has demonstrated the inextricable relationship between values and the social sciences. These fields are laden with values and as a consequence possess a unique potential for critiquing society and projecting into their practices conceptions of "the desirable," in Dewey's sense of the term. The question of values, then, is inseparable from questions surrounding the use of social critique and the deployment of normative criteria in the critical study of society and human behavior.

Given choices among the many *kinds* of norms on which critique might be based, perhaps the greatest difficulty in this practice is the challenge of establishing workable definitions of "normative criteria" and a methodology for their use. While much of critical theory is vague on this point, we have seen that Dewey and Mills worked from value-based definitions of societal problems, invoking the ideals of democracy, reason, and freedom in considering the problems of institutional life. Dewey's position, of course, was more complex and wider in scope than this short list of uncontroversial values might suggest. He appealed to a range of moral and ethical principles in critiquing existing social conditions and arrangements and in gauging the progress of democracy and reason. In any event, in the views of Dewey and Mills, social critique ultimately depended on an articulation of the historically and socially situated values most central to our lives.

Given its complexity, it is in the nature of normative thinking to contain internal inconsistencies and contradictions of its own. As

Myrdal points out, valuations are inherently unstable, "usually shifting and contradictory" (1969, 16). Values, furthermore, tend to be highly disputatious. A recurring difficulty for a culturally complex and diverse society is how to determine what/whose values are at stake. The huge panoply of values defining American society, combined with its strong ethos of individualism and personal choice, poses a potential risk of endless regression into particularism, relativism, or triviality, and at worst a decline into naked power relations.

The strong liberal orientation of most social scientists, fortunately, suggests other possible outcomes. For instance, though they might disagree with his style and method or his assessment of American society, most social scientists today, especially the more progressively minded, would likely agree with the values dear to Mills. Additionally, a reasonable amount of agreement would seem to be possible with regard to values pertaining to what many regard as inviolable rights, such as protections against unnecessary harm and suffering, guarantees of justice through due process, the preservation of human dignity, and so forth, what Myrdal calls "higher order" as opposed to "lower order" values (1969, 16–17, 67).

Dewey was joined by Mills in his conviction that science should be consciously and explicitly guided by intellectual, political, and moral norms. For both thinkers, this was a precondition for a critical, human-oriented social science. Mills, unfortunately, failed to develop the full potential and richness of Dewey's moral and ethical concerns and the place of these in science. His work, therefore, falls short of the true meaning of critique. By contrast, Dewey's pragmatism provides a groundwork for constructing a framework within which evaluative judgments could play a systematic role, involving an intersubjective and social-interactionist-based model of social critique. Such a model could build on existing critical theory to develop a more comprehensive and potentially transformative conception of society and politics. Despite overlaps between his work and that of the Frankfurt theorists, Mills's approach, less theoretical overall, has only indirect consequences for critical theory. For these reasons, the important precedents he set notwithstanding, Mills's views are less useful than Dewey's for building a scientific and socially and morally conscious sociology.

Finally, Dewey's conception of values as products of thoughtful deliberation transcending both individual desires and the objects of these desires offers a challenge to practicing social scientists to cultivate notions of the general good and strategies for implementing such notions in their work. In the spirit of Dewey's philosophy, such an effort would facilitate an integration of moral and ethical concerns into the very fabric of the social sciences, imparting to these fields a strong sense of mission and purpose.

Conclusion

The scholarly convention of a "conclusion" does not seem like an entirely appropriate ending for this book. Given the architecture of this study, the nature of the subject, and the range of topics covered, there are numerous "conclusions" that could be reached. I have touched on a series of problems and issues with no easy solutions. The reader, I hope, is left not with conclusions and straightforward answers but with a number of challenging questions.

Yet, the problems and issues raised in this book are closely interconnected, and what at times might appear to be an array of disparate topics, polemics, and themes is organized by an overall logic and rationale. Ground zero has been the critique of positivist and formalist sociology, to be sure a familiar, even timeworn exercise but one I hope to have presented from a fresh point of view. My claims about the failings of formalism and the shortcomings of conventional sociology have been rendered as symptoms of a need for a fundamental rethinking of the discipline. Guiding this task have been a number of basic questions about the purpose of sociology, its relationship to the public, and its potential as a form of social criticism. Such a task could take many forms and proceed in a number of possible directions. My own argument for a morally and politically conscious critical sociology built on the social pragmatism of John Dewey reflects my own conception of social critique and the mission of sociology.

I stand in agreement with Mills that the classical European tradition in social theory and its contemporary derivatives, wedded to social psychology, remain definitive of the field, providing a source of ideas for understanding the historical and structural problems that should be of concern to both sociologists and the public. Mills demonstrated that a sociological perspective of this kind is inherently critical, always pointing to a need for directed change based on the role of human agency in the making of history. This view puts a premium on the moral and political significance of sociological knowledge and the implications this raises for progressive social change. Accordingly, one aim of this study has been to recapitulate the legacy of Mills: his original and critical work on American society, his critique of mainstream sociology, and his aspirations for an enlightened democracy based on reason and the fruits of "the sociological imagination."

This study, however, has situated Mills's achievements in the context of American pragmatism and, specifically, the thought of Dewey. Among the manifold reasons for this particular treatment of Mills has been, first, to remind readers that American sociology was born largely of the progressive politics and moral concerns that appear in Dewey's lifelong philosophical work. The problems characterizing the historical period of sociology's formation were instrumental in defining the meaning and purpose of the discipline. I have tried to show that the intellectual and moral spirit of that time reemerges in Mills's sociology. Closely related, the symbolic interactionist school and social problems tradition that originated at Chicago in the theoretical environment shaped by Dewey and Mead have been and remain sources of critical alternatives to later trends in the field. I have suggested that the strength of Mills's work in large measure derives from his skillful integration of these Chicago influences with European theory.

Second, my discussion has attempted to show that pragmatism represents a comprehensive way out of the blind alleys of the formalism and dualistic thinking shaping postwar sociology. These trends have been at the expense of sociology's engagement with the realities of American society, inhibiting the creation of theories and research programs capable of grasping Mills's "big picture." Dewey's evolutionism, historicism, antidualism, theory of experience, conception of inquiry, and focus on human action—all are conceptual tools that could enable sociologists to discard habits of thought that unnecessarily restrict our understanding of the real nature and problems of American society, how they need to be studied, and why. A close reading of Dewey's critique of traditional Western philosophy and his effort at reconstruction brings to light a host of presuppositions behind contemporary sociological practice that became outmoded long ago with the advent of modernity and its recurrent crises. Familiarity with Dewey and pragmatism shows that mid-twentieth-century sociology took a regressive turn, against which Mills and his fellow critics reacted but from which the field has never completely recovered.

A third reason for this book's appeal to Deweyan philosophy is the importance that I believe should be given to metatheoretical thinking. Dewey's pragmatism constitutes a metatheory of society that challenges how we usually think about and practice the social sciences. It is a highly inclusive theory, premised on an epistemology and a method that reintegrate what disciplinary specialization has artificially disjoined. More than merely reaffirming the centrality of method, Dewey's work broadens our conception of method with pragmatist insights into the nature of science, knowledge, and human behavior. Dewey's metatheory, moreover, projects a picture of society and a vision of science in which questions of value are of paramount importance and in which there is a unification of scientific and moral values. His is not a sociological theory but a philosophical and theoretical program for putting the study of society on a scientific and moral foundation, bringing the two realms together in a way what enables morality and science to mutually clarify and strengthen each other within a single sphere of knowledge. As we have seen, the underlying principle of Dewey's metatheory is the unity of theory and practice. For Dewey, knowledge and action presuppose one another. For him, the conduct of science and intellectual life should be motivated by the human priorities and needs of society as a whole. Correspondingly, the moral and ethical norms governing society are subject to scientific scrutiny and are thus to be treated just as methodically as other objects of science. Finally, Dewey's metatheory rests on certain assumptions about the organization and condition of society and its institutions. Inherent in his philosophy is a model of a liberal, open, fluid, participatory, intelligently governed society. From Dewey's perspective, then, there exists a principled continuity among morality, science, and democracy.

In a world of monumental problems and crises, to propose that sociology rehabilitate itself by replacing formalism and its abstract esoterica with relevance and substance is to necessarily point sociology in a more critical and challenging direction. This suggests a need to rehabilitate the idea of social critique, which constitutes my fourth reason for focusing attention on Dewey, whose pragmatism contains many of the normative and analytical elements of this practice. In their critiques of American society, Mills and his contemporaries fell short of systematically developing this concept within a framework of social science. Nor did they indicate, except perhaps in only fragmentary and superficial ways, any links between their work and the tradition of critical theory developed by the Frankfurt School and others. Beginning with the precedents set by Mills and his critical cohorts, I have attempted to consolidate my main arguments for a substantive and critical sociology under the concept of social critique, conceived of as both an analytical method and a moral enterprise.

What needs to be explicitly affirmed, however, is the important role played by values in the practice of critique. As a normative exercise, critique presupposes a set of evaluative standards that support critical claims about a given state of affairs. Given their implicitly normative character, social theory and sociology occupy a continuum with social critique. The latter is a practice predicated on the values informing our moral judgments, expressing our beliefs about the pressing need for change in the present state of affairs and the means for achieving this goal. In their reflections on the normative character of science and social science Myrdal, Putnam, and Weber should be remembered for having established grounds for an objective conception of values, thereby putting to rest allegations that values are subjective and therefore harmful to science. I have observed a significant convergence between the views of these thinkers and those of Dewey and Mills, both of whom regarded values as foundational to social and political analysis as well as scientific inquiry. Values are both the core of social critique and the main element grounding critique in sociological analysis. Accordingly, Dewey would likely have seen sociology as taking the form of critique, serving to indicate how changes in society suggested by normative inquiry could be attained. He would have further endorsed Weber's position on the possibility of studying particular values empirically from the standpoint of their practical efficacy. In this respect, given his interest in a science of ethics, Dewey would surely have seen the appropriation of sociological principles and methods as a means of providing moral and ethical guidance to the conduct of human affairs.

This book represents an attempt to reinterpret Dewey and reframe Mills for a fresh look at the prospects of a critical sociology. This effort has involved an encounter with several of the discipline's "existential" issues. Enduring tensions between the pursuit of "knowledge for its own sake" and sociological practice in the interest of the public good and progressive change will surely not be entirely eliminated by my polemics in favor of the latter. Nor is my preference for the historicizing approaches of Dewey and Mills likely to assuage those who, with some justification, are committed to the belief that sociology is a generalizing science. At the same time, I hope to have succeeded in identifying false theoretical and methodological choices based on "either-or" thinking as opposed to the "both-and" character of Dewey's and Mills's pluralistic approaches. In this respect, the thrust of my discussion has been toward what I think are realistic strategies for a reconciliation of interactionist/interpretative/action approaches employing notions of agency and the more determinist implications of theories focused on structure and culture, an issue that only *appears* to entail two horns of a dilemma. Closely related, the antipositivist position of the entire book should not be misconstrued as a wholesale rejection of positivist methods, which should not be confused with "positivist sociology."

My allusions to the sociology of knowledge are intended to broach the possibility of reviving this neglected area of study. A subtext of my presentation of Dewey has been the suggestion that his insights into the social and historical bases and variability of ideas constitute a potential contribution to empirical studies of the social bases of knowledge. This is apparent in his sensitivity to the social conditioning of thought, his unifying of theory and practice, his evolutionism and historicism, his situating of reason in experience, and his philosophical reunification of subject and object. If it is unfortunate that Mills did not pursue his own early investigations in this area, he at least articulated the importance of the social determination of knowledge as an area of study. For him, the sociology of knowledge was an epistemological problem bearing closely on issues of validity and verifiability in the research process (Mills 1963a). In his later work, however, a sociology of knowledge frame was a continuing influence in the form of his historical and structural perspective on the psychology of the individual, specifically the formation of "character structure."

Mills makes references to Dewey's work on logic and inquiry in asserting a close relationship between the sociology of knowledge and epistemology. I would submit that a pragmatist version of the sociology of knowledge, by approaching problem solving from the standpoint of how social position and background shape and condition perception and thought, provides ground for a social "deconstruction" of social problem theorizing and research. Mills took a provocative step in this direction in his early essay on the ideological orientation of social problems researchers (1963c).

While not definitive of the larger subject of this book, the pragmatist theme of problem solving has been a recurring motif. An orientation toward substantive, historically based problems is a significant thread running from the methodological statements of Weber through the polemics of Dewey to the critical sociology of Mills. My discussion does not address the question of who controls the process of defining what constitutes a "problem." Inattention to this question is a serious weakness of pragmatism, which in its neglect of power has left the topic to thinkers like Mills. The notion of a "politics of truth" (Mills 2008), which aptly characterizes the way Mills practiced sociology, speaks to the nature of the problem. Dewey certainly was cognizant of "the problem of defining problems" in his understanding of the political and moral contexts of science, but his grasp of this process was abstract and limited.

The ideals of democracy, reason, morality, and informed opinion, always in need of vigilant protection, have been a recurring theme in my discussion of Dewey and Mills. Threats to these ideals today seem more alarming than ever, adding urgency to a call for the kind of sociology and social science implicit in Dewey's and Mills's shared vision. Much of the Frankfurt critique of domination by the "culture industry" is rapidly becoming obsolete in the face of a new set of conditions with threatening consequences for an informed public and thriving democracy. While bearing the promise of greater democratic participation, the rise of digital technology in the form of the Internet and "social media" has posed unprecedented dangers to the preservation of reason and freedom. The dark underside of this dramatic "democratization" of communication and opinion is a potential breakdown of normative standards of any kind through the encouragement of an "anything goes" mentality. Unfortunately, when everyone becomes an "authority" or "expert," no one can claim this status. The digital revolution is speedily and thoroughly disrupting accepted standards of ethical, scientific, and political judgment and behavior, not to mention our very grasp of reality and sense of what constitutes a "fact." As a consequence, adequate understanding of this technological transformation and effective means of counteracting its ill effects seem for the moment beyond reach. The implications for a critical and relevant public sociology are pressing enough to raise serious concerns about the priorities of the discipline and the promise of those ideas in the pragmatist tradition discussed in this book.

There are, of course, daunting barriers to disciplinary change. A sociology of knowledge perspective tells us that formalistic agendas tend to thrive under certain economic, occupational, and social conditions. Although academia provides considerable autonomy for social scientists, contacts outside the university are often limited to corporations, government, and other funding entities. Institutionalization and professionalization have created a discipline still too often preoccupied with its own scientific identity, organizational problems, and internal politics, all of which interfere with direct involvement in public life and civic culture. Additionally, the middle- and upper-middle-class backgrounds and positions of the majority of sociologists constitute a major disincentive for challenging the status quo. The understandable lure of career-building pursuits geared to a desired set of academic and professional goals that are personally and economically rewarding tends to encourage conformity to established disciplinary norms and paradigms. The desire for knowledge for its own sake, fears of violating conventional norms of scientific "objectivity" and "respectability," and unending funding difficulties have discouraged most sociologists from doing research that is controversial or involves recommendations for fundamental change. This is especially the case when such change is not in keeping with hegemonic social policy and the interests of the elites who shape it. In sum, these are factors posing serious obstacles to the formation of a critical and public sociology of the kind advocated by this book.

Nonetheless, change is always possible. Dewey was a pivotal figure in the transition from the nineteenth century, with its profound philosophical, social, and political developments, to the twentieth century and the promises and dangers posed by science, technology, and a capitalist market economy. He was preoccupied with the problems precipitated by these developments and devoted to theorizing a means of addressing them through a philosophy of methodical thinking and practice. His response to the uncertainties and rapidly changing environment of modernity was to transform philosophy into a form of critical engagement with the empirical world. Early American sociology refracted Dewey's conception of intellectual and scientific endeavor as serving the purpose of problem solving and social progress. As members of a discipline that began in a spirit of diagnosing, documenting, and explaining the problems of modernity, sociologists will, I hope, continue to see their work in this light, focusing their efforts on analyzing the forces that undermine the common good and the fulfillment of individual human need. In this respect, I believe the philosophy of pragmatism and the contributions of Dewey and Mills to the idea of a reformed sociology contain the intellectual means for rising to this challenge.

Notes

Chapter 1

1. My list of the "founding fathers" of sociology includes Karl Marx, Max Weber, Émile Durkheim, Alexis de Tocqueville, Georg Simmel, and Ferdinand Tonnies.

2. A clear distinction is seldom made between social and sociological theory, and the terms are often used interchangeably. I define "social theory" as a broad body of ideas and concepts related to the formation, development, and impact of modern society. The model of this is the work of the classic European social thinkers of the late nineteenth and early twentieth centuries. "Sociological theory" refers to bodies of explanatory propositions that are subject to empirical testing and verification. This type of theory is characteristic of American sociology. I strive to maintain a distinction between the two, although in some cases my statements refer to both.

3. There is a little-known alternative narrative. In the account of Aldon D. Morris (2015), whereas Robert E. Park at the University of Chicago is commonly regarded as the founder of the discipline, this official "white" version of sociology's domestic origins ignores the pioneering work of the prominent black scholar W.E.B. Du Bois at the University of Atlanta. Morris argues that through a collaboration between Park and Booker T. Washington, the story of Du Bois's Atlanta school of sociology was effectively suppressed. This story, Morris argues, needs to be brought into the open as the true version of the birth of American sociology.

4. In what follows I present only the barest outline of the direction sociology has taken in the United States. This abbreviated retrospective is intended to serve only as background for a critique of formalism. For fuller historical accounts, see Wiley 1979, Haney 2008, and Morris 2015.

5. The close connection between these thinkers is a subject unto itself. While Dewey is better known, it would appear that many of his key ideas came from Mead.

6. Although it is customary to refer to the "Chicago School," Howard S. Becker has argued that there never was a "unified and coherent body of thought" at Chicago. Rather, in the period between the 1920s and 1960s sociologists there were engaged in a variety of work reflecting a range of interests and orientations. Becker states that a more accurate characterization of the Chicagoans would be a "school of activity." See Becker 1999. Hans Joas (1993, chap. 1) offers a retrospective of the Chicago School that conveys the diversity and complexity of this early generation of sociologists, a rather complicated picture often at odds with much of the commentary on the period. The weight I place on the reformist elements of the Chicago tradition thus ignores the variety of scientific work engaged in by these early sociologists. For a comprehensive account, see Wiley 1979.

7. "Positivism" has more than one meaning. Generally, the term describes social scientists' adoption of the natural science model of causality and invariant laws within a closed universe of empirically observable "facts." Steinmetz (2005, "Introduction" and "Sociology") reduces this general conception to the search for so-called covering laws. These are general propositions believed to be universal in character and the basis for connecting the two parts of an explanation ("cause" and "effect"), an idea associated with the logical positivists. He refers to this version as "methodological positivism," as distinguished from Auguste Comte's positivism (a vision or model of "enlightened" empirical science) as well as other variants of the term. Wiley (1979) points out that positivism can also refer to the Durkheimian conception of culture and social structure as "external and constraining" forces. I use the term loosely to include these several meanings but with emphasis on a belief in the general applicability of the natural science model.

The positivist turn was closely related to a rhetoric and mythology of control. Positivism is in part a manifestation of the extension of the Enlightenment vision of control over nature to society itself and, in its worst forms, to human beings. The critique of positivism waged by members of the Frankfurt School of Critical Theory coincided with their theory of domination in advanced capitalist society. While not necessarily implicated in forms of domination as understood by this school, the growth of positivist social science, heavily supported by American administrative and political interests during and following the crises of the 1930s and 1940s, was a key strategy in the search for effective scientific means of guaranteeing social stability and order. From another angle, there is curious irony in Alvin Gouldner's claim that sociology was born of a realization of the modern problem of "alienation," a term usually associated with the Marxist tradition, in which society and culture, while human creations, take on a life of their own. In Gouldner's words, "The emerging academic social sciences thus came to conceive of society and culture as *autonomous* things: things that are independent and exist for themselves" (1970, 53). It is precisely this image of society that provides an *epistemological* rationale for positivist forms of inquiry. This is manifested in Durkheim's early positivist-oriented work in which society is conceptualized as a thing-like power over the individual.

8. The terms "formal" and "formalism" in this context have nothing to do with Georg Simmel's "formal sociology." See Tenbruck 1965.

9. See especially Merton 1957, pt. 1.

10. In this context the terms "scientism" and "scientization" refer to a sociology based on the methods of the "hard" sciences (e.g., physics and biology), a position resting on a belief in the methodological unity of natural and social science. See Steinmetz 2005 283. Thus, the word is roughly equivalent to "positivism."

11. It is perhaps no coincidence that the Society for the Study of Social Problems was founded in 1951, suggesting the need for a separate professional organization devoted to the study of social problems at a time when the discipline was moving in a different direction. This event left the American Sociological Association as the representative of the mainstream.

12. A more detailed and nuanced account of sociology's embrace of the natural science model is laid out by Steinmetz (2005, 287–309), who attributes this change to certain features of "Fordism" in postwar American society that made sociology more amenable to the principles informing natural science. For a fuller picture, see Haney, who points out that, among other factors, scientific values were being increasingly accepted by society-at-large around the same time, providing added support for a scientization of the social sciences (2008, 3).

13. This observation seems to be confirmed by the titles of roughly six of the ten articles cited in Jacobs 2015, 9–10, titles indicating a preoccupation with method.

14. Here I am using "dialectical" in the sense that Berger and Luckman (1967) use the term in *The Social Construction of Reality*.

15. The classic psychological expression of this view is found in Sigmund Freud's *Civilization and Its Discontents,* which argues that humans are destined

to be chronically unhappy, given a perpetual conflict between their innate desires and the constraining requirements of civilization.

16. In sociological discourse, modernity is often characterized as the experience of forces beyond the individual's control. While amply supported by historical evidence, such a view neglects the fact that people have likely had similar experiences throughout history. In the modern era the notion that people have lost control over their lives arose mainly from the experience of rapid change through industrial capitalism and advances in technology. The thematization of modernity as a set of uncontrollable forces coincides also with the iconic rise of the individual in Western society, seen as a volitional and self-determining agent. This theme also resonates with Enlightenment values of progress, rationality, and control over nature. In this sense, the modern question of "control" gives expression to a historically specific cultural outlook that gets reproduced in social theory. Thus, the theme of external forces always contains an ambiguity, which is often ignored in the context of modern sociology: To what extent is lack of control a historical phenomenon of "alienation" caused by the system of private property and instrumental rationality, and to what extent is seeming lack of control an existential problem, part of the human condition?

17. The concept of "reification" was introduced by the Marxist theoretician Georg Lukacs. For Lukacs, reification was the process under capitalism whereby a commodity assumes a thing-like existence independent of its producer, where "a relation between people takes on the character of a thing and thus acquires a 'phantom objectivity'" (1971, 83). We might say that sociological formalism comprises a body of concepts and postulates that have acquired the character of objects, each having a thing-like existence independent of the social world from which it originated. In a contemporary and more generic definition: "Reification means treating something as an independently existing object or reality when it does not genuinely possess this status, or when it does not have the entity-like character attributed to it" (Bloor 1997, 136).

18. During a public appearance by Talcott Parsons, the theorist of normative order, Herbert Blumer, the leading symbolic interactionist, asked the speaker, "Talcott, have you ever *seen* a norm?" This simple question exemplifies how the problem of representation has been a bone of contention between these schools of thought.

19. The error involved in what I am calling "false realism" is largely an outcome of adherence to the natural science model of inquiry, which involves a positivist denial of any difference between culture and nature.

20. See Berger and Luckman 1967.

21. The "human sciences" is a term often used by scholars who advocate an interpretive, or nonpositivist, approach to social science. The term is traceable

to the work of Wilhelm Dilthey (1961), the nineteenth-century German philosopher of hermeneutics whose classic statements on the difference between the "human" and "natural" sciences is a foundation of many interpretive approaches. For an overview of contemporary theoretical statements, see Rabinow and Sullivan 1979, 1987.

22. This is not to minimize the major contribution sociology has made to our understanding of the structural sources of human problems. The structuralist perspective has been a valuable corrective to the American tendency to perceive problems in individualistic terms. My remarks are intended to suggest only that in sociological accounts structure has often been overprivileged at the expense of action and agency.

23. In an intriguing twist on the story of the discipline's "withdrawal," David Paul Haney suggests that by the 1960s, sociologists had succeeded in painting a picture of an American mass society and culture that bred mediocrity, passivity, and conformity, in effect portraying the public as intellectually inept. More generally, the themes of alienation and anomie inherited from European social theory fed into a pessimistic view of Americans' capacity to participate meaningfully in public life. The discipline's disengagement from the public was thus also driven by a "new elitism" that grew out of sociological theory and research itself. See Haney 2008, chaps. 4 and 5.

24. As we know, formalist jargon and esoterica are a major source of the unflattering reputation sociology often suffers among other academics, intellectual workers outside of academia, and the general public.

25. Mills's statements on personal troubles and public issues, biography and history, prefigure a sociology of knowledge that was implicit in most of his work but never fully developed. Mills engaged in polemics with other theorists over the nature and status of the sociology of knowledge, primarily in response to the reception of Karl Mannheim's *Ideology and Utopia* in the United States. See Geary 2009, 30–37.

26. I am using the term "system" in a semipejorative way. My usage is not that of structural functionalism or other systems theorists. I intend the term to have both historical and quotidian meanings: historical in the sense that society as a system of interdependent parts or institutions is a *historical* product and quotidian in the sense that I want the term to reflect what ordinary people have in mind when they voice frustrations with "the system," by which they typically mean the bureaucratic system of power and wealth embodied in corporate capitalism and the modern state. Thus I am employing a historically and socially specific definition.

27. See Tawney 1948 for a classic statement of the negative consequences characterizing a society based on property rights. Acquisitiveness in our time

has taken extreme forms in (1) unrestrained individual and corporate greed, (2) obsessive consumerism, and (3) an aggressive neoliberalism seeking to privatize and marketize everything in its path.

28. See Burawoy 2005a on the notion of provincializing sociology.

Chapter 2

1. This reputation is based largely on Durkheim's foundational text, *The Rules of Sociological Method* (1982). Durkheim drew rather heavily on anthropological research. While he established the concept of sociology on the basis of its methodological procedure, this did not blind him to the role of material from related fields in documenting and supporting sociological explanation.

2. The European tradition has continued in the work of theorists such as Michel Foucault, Antonio Gramsci, and Pierre Bourdieu, who are now also "classics." In Mills's time, studies by the Frankfurt School, which reworked Marxist and Weberian themes, in several respects resonated with the concerns of Mills, especially later in his life when he gave increased attention to culture and politics.

3. Regarding differences between European and American sociologists, the macroscopic focus of European theory is perhaps related to the organization of European universities around professorships, while the more microscopic orientation of American sociologists is perhaps shaped by the departmental organization of the university. Individual professors with student followings tend to take on major historical problems, whereas the departmental pattern of American universities encourages specialized studies of particular, small-scale topics. (This observation was suggested to me by Norbert Wiley.) The microscopic orientation is likely also a reflection of a greater American interest in the individual and interpersonal/group relations.

4. Lynd employs the conventional anthropological conception of culture as "a whole way of life," as distinct from the narrower sociological conception of "a symbolic system of shared meanings." As a rule, the broader anthropological conception embraces both nonmaterial and material culture, whereas in sociology emphasis tends to be placed on nonmaterial culture, specifically beliefs, values, norms, attitudes, and so forth.

5. Sociology as a form of diagnosis is a notion that is explored in Chapter 5.

6. Certainly, there were signs of this in Mills's time in the dramatic postwar expansion of public higher education and the rise of a publishing industry providing both specialized material for an elite readership and mass circulation materials for an increasingly educated public. But there are grounds for judging Mills as having underestimated the influence of commercial mass culture,

which has grown into a gigantic, multibillion-dollar entertainment industry with dubious consequences for mass education and literacy. Indeed, these comments in *The Sociological Imagination* would seem to contradict Mills's earlier assessment in *White Collar* of the detrimental effects of mass culture and specifically his critical analysis of the destructive intellectual and political effects of the corporate mass media. Furthermore, as Haney points out (2008, 14–15), postwar sociology had already begun to portray the public as alienated and apathetic, a view consistent with Mills's portrayal in *White Collar.*

7. See the introduction in Geary 2009.

8. See Tilman 1984, 2004.

9. See discussions of this period of professionalization and critical reaction in Haney 2008, chaps. 6, 7, and 8. There is further irony in the fact that those who expressed the strongest objections to the claim that sociology had become a "science"—namely, Pitirim Sorokin and Lynd—only seemed to have had the effect of strengthening consensus around the new positivism. See Haney 2008, 124. The popularizing work of the social critics surely intensified this effect. The commentary and work of the leading proponents of formal sociology and positivist methods during this time (notably Parsons, Merton, and Lazarsfeld) would seem to corroborate such a claim.

10. The title of a chapter in Erich Fromm's *The Sane Society,* "Man in Capitalistic Society" (1955, 78), illustrates the point.

11. My discussion omits from consideration a number of prominent thinkers associated with the Frankfurt School of Critical Theory. Erich Fromm, who was connected to this group, published pioneering studies in the psychology of mass society (1941, 1947, 1955). Fromm also devoted himself to a neo-Freudian approach to the study of social character. It is significant that David Riesman studied under Fromm and mentions in the preface to *The Lonely Crowd* the influence of two works of Fromm, *Escape from Freedom* (1941) and *Man for Himself* (1947), which Riesman characterizes as "influential models in the application of socially oriented psychoanalytic characterology to problems of historical change" (Riesman, Glazer, and Denny 1961, xiv). Herbert Marcuse wrote Freudian- and Marxist-oriented critiques of advanced capitalism, the best known of which was *One Dimensional Man* (1964). Mention need hardly be made of the work of the leading members of the school, Max Horkheimer and Theodor Adorno, whose essay "The Culture Industry: Enlightenment as Mass Deception" (1969), originally published in 1944, is the classic theoretical critique of American mass culture. Also, Adorno was a member of the research team that produced *The Authoritarian Personality* (1964), a monumental example of scholarly psychological interest in social character following the war, in this case provoked by the rise of European fascism. Leo Lowenthal contrib-

uted to the Frankfurt project through his sociological studies of literature and character structure. The gloomy prognoses of the Frankfurt thinkers, who in a "one-dimensional" manner saw only new forms of domination and manipulation in advanced capitalist society, have since been widely challenged (see, for example, Kellner 1983). Mills's *White Collar* (1956) echoes many of the Frankfurt scholars' concerns. Their work constitutes an important chapter in the story of critical psychological and cultural writings on postwar America. Finally, any characterization of this period would be incomplete without mention of noted critics of mass culture such as Dwight MacDonald, Irving Howe, and other figures in the circle of New York intellectuals during Mills's time and with whom he had ties. See Geary 2009, Haney 2008, and Horowitz 1983. See also the edited collection titled *Mass Culture* (Rosenberg and White 1957), which contains an assortment of critical essays by Mills's contemporaries.

12. Strictly speaking, "personality" and "character" refer to different aspects of the individual, but in the social criticism literature the terms tend to be used interchangeably or at least in closely related ways.

13. As Daniel Geary has pointed out, the study by Gerth and Mills was part of a trend in the 1940s toward social psychological inquiries precipitated by the rise of totalitarianism. In addition, under the influence of Talcott Parsons and through a growing American awareness of European social theory, social scientists at this time were taking up a strong interest in social structure (see Chapter 1). Mills was also a part of this trend, but unlike most others in the discipline, he stressed the importance of a historical perspective. See Geary 2009, 50–53. The popularity of Freudian theory during this same period partially accounts for the tendency of scholars to use psychological categories in their investigations. Regarding the vogue in "national character" studies during the same period, Mills did not regard his work on social character as belonging to this body of research, which has subsequently fallen into disrepute.

14. The emergence of consumer culture is a historically complex topic, as it occurred over a long period of time, and it would be a mistake to date the phenomenon to Veblen's era. See Dunn 2008.

15. For a fuller discussion of Galbraith's observation, see Dunn 2008, 40–41. A notable feature of his argument is its implicit support of the notion of capitalist "need creation" set forth by members of the Frankfurt School (particularly Herbert Marcuse) and their followers. Galbraith locates the phenomenon not in the Madison Avenue sales apparatus but in the economic logic of capitalism itself. What his argument overlooks, however, is the fact that production decisions are largely an outcome of market research, whose purpose it is to make preproduction determinations of consumer tastes and preferences. While the status and relevance of market research findings and how they are

interpreted and used remain murky, they nevertheless constitute an important part of our understanding of consumer behavior.

16. Whyte's observations and his contemporaries' emphasis on conformity provide an interesting contrast to the later book by Philip Slater, *The Pursuit of Loneliness* (1970). As the title implies, Slater attributes what he sees as the troubling problems of American life during this period to an *excessive individualism,* effectively inverting the dominant view of other social critics of the time. I would submit that the two views are not incompatible. Without paying any attention to structural factors that are its cause (with the exception of lip service to "institutional analysis" at the end of the book), Slater talks only about the socially isolating effects of the ideology of competitive individualism. One might argue that the consequences of this ideology are partially responsible for pressures toward group conformity, independently of the organizational forces discussed by Whyte. In any event, while offering a provocative array of insights, Slater's arguments are almost wholly cultural and psychological in nature, resting exclusively on voluntarist premises and a view that blames the victim: Americans' problems are traceable to the actors themselves.

17. Wasting no time introducing this image of the new middle class, Mills in the introduction to *White Collar* refers to "the decline of the independent individual and the rise of the little man in the American mind" (1956, xii).

18. See Adorno 1975.

19. See Geary 2009. In his thoughtful and judicious assessment of *White Collar,* Geary among other things contextualizes the book in Mills's politics. According to Geary, the book is best understood in terms of Mills's trajectory from an earlier belief in the possibility of labor developing into a progressive political force in the United States to a state of "political disillusionment." The conservative implications he saw in the formation of a white-collar middle class subjected to the stifling effects of bureaucratic control and mass culture caused Mills to lose hope (ibid., 108–125). Geary also presents an extensive comparison of *White Collar* and *The Lonely Crowd,* which he regards as highly similar works that captured the same social and psychological syndromes in postwar America. In a journal review, Riesman wrote approvingly of Mills's study, despite the limitations he saw in the overly simplistic and unfavorable portrayal of the white-collar worker (ibid., 135–142).

20. A book that in certain respects complements the critique of 1950s America presented in *White Collar* but reaches far beyond it is the scorching attack by Paul Goodman, *Growing Up Absurd* (1956). Goodman indicts not the organization or the world of white-collar work but what he calls the "Organized System," which he sees as a concentration of power that misappropriates society's resources in a way that destroys values and common sense. His main

concern is with the plight of disaffected youth, whom he believes the Organized System deprives of a chance to grow up sane and healthy.

21. The major exception to this was Mills's study *The Power Elite* (1959).

22. Perhaps the main exception is the work of Riesman, Glazer, and Denny (1961).

23. *White Collar*, for instance, "concentrated its attention almost exclusively on how social structure shaped character" (Geary 2009, 133). Mills devoted little effort to showing the role of human behavior in the constitution of social structure or indicating how actors could shape structure and history, a reflection of his growing political pessimism by the time he wrote the book.

24. Arguing that people unsuccessfully seek social esteem in their nonwork lives as compensation for workplace alienation, Mills is not clear and consistent enough to convincingly explain the dynamics of this predicament. Also, while providing some grounds for his claim of alienation in both work and leisure, he overlooks aspects of both that might be sources of esteem and self-fulfillment. His one-sided analysis thus seems to preclude any possibility of white-collar workers finding genuine meaning and identity on the job.

25. Riesman took an especially strong interest in Veblen's work, and Mills was indebted to the economist (Riesman 1960; Riesman 1993, 374–401; Horowitz 1983, 8).

26. The idea of contradiction that surfaced in Veblen's critique was subsequently marginalized in favor of the vague and more neutral sociological term "cultural lag." The latter is an imprecise concept loosely referring to maladjustments between nonmaterial culture and the changing material base of society, in which the former lags behind the latter. Veblen's writings on the social dysfunctions of industrial society have led some authors to characterize him as a cultural lag theorist, effectively watering down his trenchant criticism of turn-of-the-century American capitalism. The term "cultural lag" was coined in 1922 by William Ogburn (1966). See Tilman 2007.

27. Of course, this tradition of criticism never entirely disappeared. Social scientists with journalistic and generalist bents have continued to make a mark on the field despite the reigning orthodoxy. Some familiar examples are *Habits of the Heart* by Robert Bella et al.; numerous works by Barbara Ehrenreich, including *Fear of Falling: The Inner Life of the Middle Class* and *Nickel and Dimed: On (Not) Getting By in America; The Managed Heart: Commercialization of Human Feeling* and *The Second Shift*, both by Arlie Russell Hochschild; *Haven in a Heartless World: The Family Besieged* and *The Culture of Narcissism: American Life in an Age of Diminishing Expectations*, both by Christopher Lasch; and many others. Fortunately, such best-selling commentators on contemporary American life have kept the intellectual and human sides of social science alive.

Chapter 3

1. Grounds for the rise of conflict theory had already been laid in the 1950s with the publication in paperback of Lewis Coser's *The Functions of Social Conflict* and Ralf Dahrendorf's *Class and Class Conflict in Industrial Society.* However, it was mainly the surge of interest in Marxism that drew attention to this model. The case of Coser is interesting, as his study of conflict could be read as an astute defense of the functionalist paradigm.

2. In the late 1960s, opposition to the positivist consensus and its conservative overtones was a feature of a number of peripheral "grassroots" movements connected to university communities, including the New Left, the so-called counterculture, and second-wave feminism, all of which were in part expressions of opposition to prevailing academic paradigms and doctrines in many fields of study.

3. While at the University of Texas Mills earned a master's degree in "American philosophy and modern logic," concentrating on the work of "Charles S. Peirce and G. H. Mead." His "key teacher was George V. Gentry, a student of Mead's" (Mills 2000, 80).

4. See Tilman 1984 for an informative treatment of the influence of pragmatism, and especially John Dewey, on Mills and his work.

5. For historical perspectives on pragmatism, see West 1989, which finds its beginnings in Ralph Waldo Emerson, and Menand 2001, which situates the birth of pragmatism in the formation of "The Metaphysical Club." See Jay 2005, chap. 7, for a detailed account of the early sources of pragmatist ideas, especially those of James.

6. See Brinkmann 2013, 5–8, for a discussion of affinities between Dewey's thought and postmodernism. I stress the importance of a comparison only to *philosophical* and to some extent political postmodernism. The founding pragmatists would be dubious of other varieties. Ironically, with the exception of its qualified use among some contemporary scholars, the term "postmodern" has acquired so many meanings as to become rather useless.

7. This, of course, has hardly been a matter of increasing economic democracy, with the exception of the affluent 1950s and 1960s. Regarding the relationship between pragmatism and social change, James and Dewey offer interesting cases. The teachings of James resonated with much of the educated public, in part due to his gifts as a speaker but also as a result of his close, sympathetic attention to the variety of beliefs, faiths, and experiences of the "common man." Dewey has been widely known not only for his active participation in civic culture and political life but also, most notably, for his educational theories, which have had a wide and democratizing influence. One could read

Dewey's whole philosophy as based on the notion of a democratization of knowledge and reason. For a sociology-of-knowledge approach to these thinkers that explores their social backgrounds, positions, achievements, and deficiencies, see Mills's published dissertation (1964). On democratization, see Mannheim 1956, pt. 3.

8. See Sydney Hook's 1995 biography of Dewey for a discussion of the latter's political involvements and impact on public and intellectual life.

9. I quote Bacon's formulation for its clarity, as opposed to the original statement by Peirce.

10. Richard Bernstein asserts, "The point of the pragmatic maxim is to relate thought and judgment to human conduct" (2010, 45). He claims that for Peirce "action" is singular, whereas "conduct" is general. According to Bernstein, the function of the procedure, then, is *clarification* of our "habits of conduct and the inferential consequences of our thoughts and judgments" (ibid., 46). For Bernstein, this comes into view when we look at the maxim from the standpoint of Peirce's theory of signs. For Peirce, thought is impossible without signs (we might say more generally "language"). It is noteworthy that in the context of a discussion of Peirce's semiotics Bernstein makes an explicit connection between the maxim—a philosophical scientific proposition—and human conduct. This implies a deep association in Peirce's thinking between his scientific concerns and the conduct of social life. Such a connection becomes explicit in Dewey's work.

11. Regarding James's reorientation of pragmatism toward the psychology of the individual, it is worth noting the subtitle of this book, "A Study of Human Nature."

12. For a comprehensive biography of the life of James that addresses this and related issues, see Richardson 2006.

13. James's embrace of "the flow of experience" has an obvious affinity with the "intuitive" philosophy of the Frenchman Henri Bergson and specifically the latter's concepts of *élan vital* and *durée*. The two men were personally acquainted, and James spent a considerable amount of time in France, becoming a highly popular lecturer with the French public. See Richardson 2006.

14. Given its focus on subjective experience, James's thought is often portrayed as a precursor of phenomenology.

15. See Featherstone 1972 for a retrospective and insightful interpretation of the evolution of Dewey's thought.

16. See the observations in Weber 1958b and Habermas 1984 on the rise of instrumental rationality and its manifestation in the modern differentiation of value spheres.

17. See Mills 1964, chap. 20, for a discussion. The quotation marks around "behaviorism" are intended to problematize this term in light of its several

meanings. Dewey critiqued the prevailing stimulus-response behaviorism of his time while formulating his own behaviorism, one that acknowledged the self-reflexive, thought-based, and "organic" character of behavioral processes. See Dewey 1896.

18. Its focus on experience was a chief target of Durkheim's attack on pragmatism. As evident in his lectures on the subject (Durkheim 1983), Durkheim developed a sympathetic interest in pragmatism toward the end of his life, one of a number of signs that his theorizing was leading him in the direction of symbolic interactionism (Stone and Farberman 1967). While supportive of pragmatism's criticism of the excesses of rationalism, Durkheim complained that its conflation of "experience" and "reality" erased the latter, thus undermining rational thought and any foundation for "truth." Attempting to retain the idea of an objective world "out there," Durkheim rejected Dewey's merging of subjectivity and objectivity and James's notion of "radical empiricism," which claimed that nothing existed outside of experience. Despite his compelling defense of the distinction between subject and object, Durkheim actually misconstrues Dewey's ideas and intent. A clarification of Dewey's thought would most likely have dispelled much of Durkheim's misperception of pragmatist principles by reasserting pragmatists' firm belief in the social foundations of thought and action, a thoroughly Durkheimian idea.

19. The attention I devote to the impact of Hegel and Darwin serves my interest in the social aspects of Dewey's philosophy and should not minimize the important role played by Dewey's encounter with behaviorist psychology. His critique of this tradition in "The Reflex Arc Concept in Psychology" (1896) is the key to Dewey's whole reconceptualization of human behavior and in certain respects prefigures his theory of experience.

20. One might think of Dewey's entire philosophy as in part a long battle against the chronic mistake of taking abstractions for reality.

21. While Hegel and Darwin are obvious sources of the temporal dimension in Dewey's thought, Bergson should be mentioned as contributing to the prominence of the concept of temporality in nineteenth-century and early twentieth-century philosophy and thus also likely having an influence on Dewey.

22. The main chapters of this 1932 publication comprise the Carus Lectures that Mead delivered to a meeting of the American Philosophical Association at Berkeley in 1930. Interestingly, this book contains "Prefatory Remarks" by Dewey in which he praises Mead's contribution to the field, commenting particularly on his notions of "emergence" and "sociality," key concepts in Mead's never fully completed philosophy.

23. Jay points out that late in life Dewey conceded that "historical obstacles" had "prevented understanding of my use of 'experience.'" Dewey says

he would have instead used the term "culture." Further complicating matters, in his last published work, *Knowing and the Known* (Dewey and Bentley 1960), Dewey states that "trans-action" might have been the preferable term for conveying what he meant by "experience." See Jay 2005, 298–299.

24. In Dewey's conception, "means" and "ends" are thoroughly relative terms. In the ongoing process of experimental inquiry into problems and acts of adjustment to a continually changing environment, means can turn into ends and vice versa in an extended chain of adaptation-based action. In other words, knowledge and action are never completed or finished, "final ends" never achieved in a world that is constantly changing. See Dewey's 1939 *Theory of Valuation*.

25. See Hook 1995, chap. 5.

26. In Menand's interpretation, "pragmatism is an account of the way people think—the way they come up with ideas, form beliefs, and reach decisions" (2001, 351).

27. Instead of "pragmatism," Dewey preferred instead the terms "naturalism," "experimentalism," or "instrumentalism" (Brinkmann 2013, 19). In the preface to *Logic,* Dewey says, "The word 'Pragmatism' does not, I think, occur in the text" (Dewey 2013, 4). By the time he wrote this massive volume, late in life (it was published in 1938), "so much misunderstanding and relatively futile controversy [had] gathered about the word" that he chose to "avoid" it altogether (ibid.). He admits, however, that "in the proper interpretation of 'pragmatic,' namely, the function of consequences as necessary tests of the validity of propositions, *provided* these consequences are operationally instituted and are such as to resolve the specific problems *evoking* the operations, the text that follows is thoroughly pragmatic" (ibid.; italics in original).

28. In this and other texts, Dewey leaves himself open to a number of criticisms. By speaking of means and ends in the abstract he can be easily attacked for moral relativism. We need to know whose and what means and ends are at stake. Additionally, his emphasis on the "instrumental" and "natural" as components of an experimental approach seems to omit consideration of the inner life and the place of contemplation and reflection in the way humans think.

29. Bernstein claims that a number of studies of the pragmatists "show the striking differences between pragmatism and positivism" (1999, 168).

30. It is not entirely clear what Mills means by this comment. Generally, Mills tends to misinterpret Dewey's use of "the biological." See Dewey 1960b, chap. 9.

31. Dewey devotes chapter 10 of *Knowing and the Known* (first published in 1949) to a clarification of what he sees as the similarities and differences between science and common sense.

32. See Jay 2005, 298–299.

33. See Weber 1947, 87–157.

34. An example of Blumer's appreciative references to Dewey is the importance he attached to Dewey's "Reflex Arc" article, which Blumer often referred to in his writings and teaching. See Blumer 1969. Blumer believed that Dewey's critique of the stimulus-response model was fundamental to an understanding of Meadian theory and laid important groundwork for the concept of symbolic interaction.

35. Blumer's "formative interaction" brings to mind Durkheim's notion of "social emergence." See Blumer 1969, chap 3.

36. See Blumer 1969, chaps. 1 and 2.

37. For major statements on agency and structure, see Giddens 1979, 1984; Bourdieu 1977; Hays 1994; and Archer 1982.

38. See Dewey 1957, pt. 1, "The Place of Habit in Human Conduct."

39. See Mills 1963b, pt. 4, esp. "Language, Logic, and Culture," "Situated Actions and Vocabularies of Motive," and "Methodological Consequences of the Sociology of Knowledge."

Chapter 4

1. We find this view scattered throughout Dewey's writings, but it appears most fully in his aesthetic theory set forth in *Art as Experience* (1958b).

2. For a comprehensive retrospective on the development of instrumental rationality from the perspective of the Frankfurt School, see Jay 2016.

3. Plato's scheme dividing the world of ideas or "perfect forms" from the imperfections of the real world of "things" can be thought of as the classic philosophical expression of this dichotomy.

4. This is elaborated in Dewey's theory of logic.

5. See, for example, Bernstein 1999, Galgan 1988, Rytina and Loomis 1970, and Tilman 1984.

6. The term "public intellectual," of which Dewey was perhaps the first best-known example, was first introduced by Russell Jacoby (1987) and has been in circulation, especially in discussions of Mills and his contemporaries, ever since. Regarding the political controversy surrounding Dewey, while Dewey was initially a liberal reformer, in the aftermath of World War I and amid growing signs of worldwide economic and political crisis, his politics became more socialist. This corresponds to Richard Rorty's observation in the introduction to Sydney Hook's study of Dewey (his former professor) that Dewey and Hook were "anti-Communist social democrats" (Hook 1995, xv). Indeed, the list of Dewey's involvements in the social and political causes of this period, including his defense of Leon Trotsky during the Moscow Trials, is quite extensive. See chapter 8 of Hook 1995 for an informative and sympathetic discussion of Dewey's politics.

7. The concept of "praxis," which originated with the Greeks, has appeared in the work of a host of philosophers, Marxist and non-Marxist alike. Given Dewey's immersion in an Americanized Hegelian tradition during a time of rising popularity for socialism in the West, resemblances between this aspect of his philosophy and the Marxist notion of praxis are hardly surprising.

8. Hans Sluga (2014) draws a distinction between two types of political theory, the "normative" and the "diagnostic," generally approving of the modern trend he finds away from the former toward the latter. This quote indicates that Dewey, in basic agreement with Sluga, finds fault with normative theorizing while his promotion of experimental method and empirically based knowledge is more suggestive of Sluga's conception of the diagnostic mode of thought.

9. The scholar and teacher Ernest Becker once distinguished between "passive empirical" and "active ideational" modes of thought (personal lecture notes), a distinction that parallels Dewey's conception of the difference between static concepts on the one hand and agentic and processual concepts on the other.

10. These passages are difficult to interpret. While it is apparent what Dewey is driving at, his remarks about concept formation constitute one of his more puzzling arguments. It is not at all clear what his concept of the State, or any other entity, would actually look like. Here, Dewey's thinking encounters a logical obstacle: Concepts by their very nature serve a *stabilizing* function, they fix in place what would otherwise remain a chaos of perceptions and representations. The essential function of concepts is to provide the mind with logical structure in order to capture and make sense of a complex and fluid reality. Here, Dewey seems unwilling to concede the difficulties involved in representing or theorizing "process," a key principle of his philosophy. Moreover, in the absence of a tentative formal definition, it would be difficult to distinguish between what is a state and what is not a state, or how we might be able to decide the difference between a "good" state and a "bad" one. If in these quotes, on the other hand, Dewey is referring to the fact that concepts as practical tools of explaining and understanding the world are always subject to theoretical and empirical revision, than his statements seem more acceptable.

11. Explicitly defining thought in terms of human activity as opposed to contemplative and abstract reasoning, Dewey states, "Intelligence as distinct from the older conception of reason, is inherently involved in action." Attacking another conventional dualism, he adds, "Moreover, there is no opposition between it and emotion. There is such a thing as passionate intelligence" (1934, 79).

12. In a rather uncharacteristic concession to the unpredictable results of human action, Dewey comments on the "'accidental' relation in institutional

development" involving "consequences that . . . were not foreseen or intended" (Dewey 1934, 75–76). This acknowledgment of the unintended/unanticipated consequences of action is a significant corrective to the impression Dewey tends to leave that rational, purposive conduct guarantees the achievement of desired ends. At the same time, one can argue that this familiar sociological concept is of a piece with notions of fallibility and theoretical revision.

13. Hegel paved the way for this facet of Dewey's thinking. Jay comments that Hegel "embraced a dynamic philosophy of relationality in which subjects and objects were mutually constituting" (2016, 63).

14. See "The Supremacy of Method" in Dewey 1960b.

15. See reference to this distinction in note 9 above.

16. An interesting convergence between Dewey and Weber is observable in Mills's work. While Dewey stressed problem solving, Weber claimed that every scientific field is defined by the problems it studies (Weber 1949, 68). Mills's insistent focus on problems reflects both influences.

17. See, especially, Dewey's *The Public and Its Problems* (1954), *Human Nature and Conduct* (1957), *Freedom and Culture* (1963), and *Liberalism and Social Action* (2000).

18. Dewey was vague on the specifics of agency. His early writings seemed to favor the actions of individuals in guiding society toward a better future. In a later, seemingly less optimistic mood, he indicated support for collective, organized action. In his criticisms of Dewey, Mills carelessly misses this change of position, arguing that the logic of Dewey's belief in the power of intelligence in shaping change is a mandate for an individualistic conception of agency as opposed to the actions of organizations or movements.

19. Despite the generic character of Dewey's use of the word "change," put in context it is apparent that the term refers to social change. Since for Dewey everything human was social in character, it follows that "society" was Dewey's implicit reference point when talking about change.

20. This set of concerns is most evident in *White Collar* (1956).

21. The relevant books are, in order of appearance, *The New Men of Power* (first published 1948), *White Collar* (first published 1951), and *The Power Elite* (first published 1956). See Geary 2009, 151. As Geary notes, since the first book was a study of labor leaders, it was not strictly speaking about the working class (2009, 249n25).

22. The emphasis on particularity as against generality is another striking instance of parallels between Dewey and Weber. The latter used the term "historical individual" (a particular cultural and social configuration—e.g., the modern money economy) to describe what he believed was the proper object of social science investigation (Weber 1949, 79). See Chapter 5. This

was Mills's approach in his work on contemporary power relationships and the "new" middle-class society.

23. Mills developed his notion of cultural apparatus over a period of time in writings that were never published in book form. Late in his career Mills widened his identification of potential change agents to include not only traditional intellectuals but also "cultural workers." Implementing this expanded category, he defined the cultural apparatus as "all those organizations and *milieux* in which artistic, intellectual and scientific work goes on" and "all the means by which such work is made available to small circles, wider publics, and to great masses" (from Mills 1958, 73, qtd. in Geary 2009, 190; see also "The Cultural Apparatus," Mills 1963, 405–422). This turn to the realm of symbolic meanings was a gesture in the direction of cultural politics, a move that connected Mills to the American New Left of the 1960s, the British cultural Marxists, and the Frankfurt School. One might say this concept was Mills at his dialectical best. On the one hand there were moments of optimism about the possibility of those in the cultural apparatus becoming agents of radical social change; on the other hand Mills pessimistically saw the cultural apparatus falling into the hands of the corporate economy and the nation-state, becoming a tool of manipulation and conformity in the form of mass culture and its correlative, mass apathy. This part of his theory has affinities with the later argument of Jürgen Habermas in his 1989 publication, *The Structural Transformation of the Public Sphere,* in which the public disintegrates into a mass of private individuals beholden to consumer society and its corporate bidders. Later in this work, Mills struck a more optimistic tone, drawing on the pragmatist notion of the "constitutive power of language" as a basis for an "autonomous" cultural apparatus (Geary 2009, 193) and the possible formation of new forms of consciousness supporting liberatory change. This view invites comparison to Habermas's work on communicative action (1984), which draws on pragmatist theory for the purpose of rehabilitating a liberatory concept of reason. See Jay 2016 and Antonio 1989.

24. My discussion of their differences is based on commentary on Mills's political criticisms of Dewey in Tilman (1984, chap. 8; 2004, 212–217) and Geary (2009, chap. 2).

25. Mills makes the mistake of taking Dewey's biological model of action too literally and reductively. Dewey saw action and evolution partly in terms of interactions between humans and nature, partly in terms of interactions among humans themselves (i.e., social relations). Mills apparently failed to see how Dewey wove these dimensions together in a complex picture of social evolution. Generally, Mills fails to grasp the extent to which the biological imagery in Dewey's writings serves to model society and social change on the *idea* of Darwinian adaptation. It is obvious that Dewey invokes Darwinism,

sometimes by analogy, sometimes metaphorically, to characterize the *nature* of the social process.

26. These Deweyan ideas, and what Dewey meant by them, have been the object of endless controversy. According to Joseph Featherstone, "The ambiguity in the term 'adjustment' lay in the fact that Dewey meant two nearly opposite things by it. He meant a passive adaptation to the social environment, and he meant mastery and control of it" (1972, 27). Both interpretations leave unanswered the political connotations of Dewey's Darwinian language and how Dewey himself understood these terms theoretically and practically.

27. The debate here would seem to revolve around the distinction between "adjustment" and "transformation." Both are vague and ambiguous terms requiring definition, context, and reference points. In fact, it is not entirely clear that these terms refer to mutually exclusive ideas. Such debate in certain respects alludes to the difference between "reform" and "revolution," a much clearer distinction. (Neither Dewey nor Mills advocated the latter.)

28. According to Hook, Dewey at this time acknowledged the need for "reforming . . . the institutional scheme of things" (1995, 165), implying the kind of organized action in the interest of institutional and structural change advocated by social democrats and, apparently, Mills himself.

29. This radical turn in Dewey's politics was undoubtedly a response to the Great Depression.

30. Tilman is probably right to characterize Mills's objections to Dewey's liberalism as historically misplaced insofar as they were more applicable to the liberalism of Mills's own time.

31. Given Dewey's view of purposive action as entailing situationally based methods of experimental inquiry, one interpretation is that Dewey himself regarded humans as "craftsmen." See the discussion in the section titled "Man as Craftsman" in Bernstein 1999, 213–219.

32. "Professional sociology" is in practice roughly but not entirely equivalent to what I mean by "formal" or "formalistic" sociology.

33. This seems to be what Burawoy in part has in mind when he refers to a "*sociology of publics*" (2005b, 8, italics in original).

Chapter 5

1. It is seldom clear what the overused term "value-free sociology" actually means. For instance, in his criticism of this notion Alvin Gouldner (1962) mostly limited himself to Weber's statements about fact-value separation in "Science as a Vocation" (1958c), his famous lecture warning against personal bias in the classroom. Gouldner's narrow definition of the problem ignores Weber's more elaborated discussion in "'Objectivity' in Social Science and So-

cial Policy" (1949), which outlines the multiple and complex ways that values enter into sociological inquiry. In his discussion of fact and value, even Putnam (2002, 63) ignores this essay and as a result overlooks Weber's intricate dissection of the problem.

2. Gunnar Myrdal made a point of using the term "valuations" rather than "values," stating that the "subjectivity" of the former term keeps actors in the picture and more accurately describes how values function in the social sciences. As he indicated, people hold "values" (objects) but engage in "valuations" (a form of behavior). See Myrdal 1969 and commentary by his daughter in the introduction to a reissued publication of volume 1 of *An American Dilemma* (Myrdal 2009).

3. This is true notwithstanding the frequent cultural and subcultural differences between researchers and subjects.

4. Perhaps the best-known example of this in sociology is the strong conservative overtones of Talcott Parsons's version of functionalism. He employs some of these same terms while claiming that society is a "normative order" and a "system seeking equilibrium," a theory not so faintly attributing "normalcy" and legitimacy to the prevailing value system and existing order. See Parsons 1951. Some have gone further, arguing that even philosophical and methodological positions in social science are ideological in character. It could be argued, for example, that as an approach to social scientific inquiry, positivism, by presupposing that the social world is governed by laws akin to those of nature, in effect underwrites a belief that existing social arrangements are "natural" and therefore "necessary" or "immutable." Positivist sociology thus harbors a conservative message. See Shaw 1973.

5. Despite their embeddedness in language, values are always to some degree transparent and subject to scrutiny. Nonetheless, acknowledging that language itself is an inescapable source of valuation is a reminder that, as Wittgenstein (2009) taught us, language is the arbiter of the limits of our knowledge and understanding of the world. These limits, however, can be discerned and taken into account in our theories and practices.

6. For a fuller discussion of Putnam, see Bernstein 2010, chap. 7.

7. Weber's well-known analytical constructs of economy, religion, bureaucracy, and authority types are examples of this method of abstractly "modeling" historical types of sociocultural phenomena on the basis of their salient characteristics. See Weber 1947 and other essays in this same book.

8. Certainly, making one's own values explicit and open to inspection allows for stronger claims to "objectivity." Aside from this basic rationale for open expression of values, however, with the partial exception of Weber's methodological prescriptions, none of the thinkers examined here offers use-

ful guidance on the form this kind of self-reflexivity might take and how it can be achieved in practice.

9. For further discussion of values in science, see Bell 2008, esp. chap. 2.

10. Among the many expressions of Dewey's historicism, this quote from *Experience and Nature* is unequivocal: "Aside from mathematics, all knowledge is historic" (1958b, 163).

11. As indicated in previous chapters, the social problems orientation of the Chicago School as well as Dewey's reformist-minded philosophy and politics were manifestations of this early twentieth-century environment of moral concern. It is also worth recalling that in its early years many entrants to the field of sociology were Protestants from professionally religious backgrounds. From its inception, the field was colored by moral and reformist impulses, and the joining of religious/moral interests to sociology, seen as a scientific instrument of social amelioration, was a commonplace response to fears of social and moral decay.

12. Parallel to Durkheim's thesis that morality changes with changing social conditions, Dewey's historicism led him to a historically relative conception of values. As an example, see chapter 3 of his *Liberalism and Social Action* (2000). Durkheim's and Dewey's conception of the social and historical relativity of morals brings to mind Weber's notion that values function in historically specific ways and that empirical science therefore can analyze value positions in terms of their validity or viability for a given set of historical or social circumstances.

13. This is another of several Durkheimian themes in Dewey. Both thinkers responded to the modern crisis of religion by turning to theories of morality and education, specifically their mutually interrelated functions in socialization of the individual and maintenance of the social bond. Dewey and Durkheim both believed that education was the primary means of secularizing morality. See Dewey 1934 and Durkheim 1956, 1961. See also Dill 2007. Given Durkheim's interest in pragmatism (1983), similarities between his and Dewey's concerns and ideas are worth further exploration. See Joas's comparison and contrast of Durkheim and pragmatism (1993, chap. 2). See also Dewey 1957, pt. 4. In addition, see "The Durkheim and Dewey Page," by Andrea Nagy, at studymore.org.uk/xnagy.htm.

14. See Dewey 1966a, "Introduction."

15. While perhaps not germane to his purposes, how Dewey actually defined "morality" remains an open question, although providing a formal definition would have been inconsistent with his philosophical principles. Accordingly, his notion of morality and ethics remained "situational." See Brinkmann 2013, 111–112.

16. See Pappas 1998 for a discussion of Dewey's ethics. Moral concerns were so important to him that, according to Sydney Hook, "Dewey was led to his logical investigations as a result of his attempt to provide a scientific foundation for moral judgments" (1995, 88).

17. For an extensive analysis of the concept of objective value from a different perspective, see Georg Simmel's monumental 1990 study, *The Philosophy of Money*.

18. "Work in social science has always been accompanied by problems of evaluation" (Mills 1961, 76).

19. See Gerth and Mills 1964 on the role of values in the social psychology of the individual.

20. The literature covering this tradition is extensive. On the topic of immanent critique, see Antonio 1981 and Stahl 2014. On the Frankfurt School, see Jay 1973.

21. Referring to "the technical and economic conditions of machine production" (Weber 1958a, 181) dominating modern life, the term "iron cage," which appears on this same page, was coined by Talcott Parsons in his translation of Weber's study of religion and capitalism.

22. Sluga presents a probing analysis of the origins and development of diagnostic thinking, which he counterposes to the "normative tradition" in political theory. He sees the diagnostic mode of thought emerging with Marx and Nietzsche and appearing later in the work of thinkers like Weber, Carl Schmitt, the Frankfurt theorists, Hannah Arendt, and Foucault.

23. "Pathology" and other medical metaphors are scattered throughout Durkheim's early work, which relies heavily on terminology and models from natural science. Social problems, from Durkheim's perspective, are manifestations of an "abnormality" in the "social body." On anomie, see Durkheim 1951. In a classic essay, "Social Structure and Anomie," Robert K. Merton, who was later to become identified with the sociological mainstream, employs the anomie concept in a Marxist-sounding critical argument about the structural obstacles to upward mobility in American society. In a parallel with the practice of immanent critique, Merton points to the contradiction between the cultural goal of monetary success and a lack of economic opportunity. See Merton 1957, 131–160. For an informative discussion of the medical model of diagnosis, see Sluga 2014, 33–40.

24. There is, of course, a functionalist dimension to Marx's theory of capitalism. He attempts to analyze how this system becomes dysfunctional *as a system* as part of his wider theory of social change in which a combination of structural breakdown in the economy and collective worker opposition to the ruling class leads to human emancipation. See Marx 1906 and 1959.

25. Although Mills (1961) uses the term "institutional contradiction" on the first page of *The Sociological Imagination* (unfortunately without explaining what this meant), the postwar critics generally did not avail themselves of the concept.

26. The social dislocation, impoverishment, and resulting discontent of working people in the "older" economy of the Midwest were major factors in the populist backlash against Washington politics and policies that elected Donald Trump to the presidency in the 2016 election.

27. See Kadlec 2006 for documentation of neo-Marxist hostility toward pragmatism. As she indicates, Frankfurt School member Max Horkheimer, a severe critic of Dewey, in *Eclipse of Reason* identified pragmatism with "vulgar positivism" (Kadlec 2006, 253). It would seem that nothing could be further from the truth. See also Jay 1973 and Joas 1993, chap. 4.

28. In Bernstein's words, Dewey "advocated a conception of philosophy in which it would become a form of social criticism" (1999, 201).

29. For representative criticisms of Frankfurt School critical theory, see Kadlec 2006 and Kellner 1983.

30. For more detailed treatments of pragmatism as critical theory, see Antonio 1989, Kadlec 2006, and Shalin 1992.

References

Adorno, T. W. 1975. Culture Industry Reconsidered. *New German Critique* 6:12–19.

Adorno, T. W., Else Frenkel-Brunswik, Daniel J. Levinson, and R. Nevitt Sanford. 1964. *The Authoritarian Personality,* Parts 1 and 2. New York: John Wiley and Sons.

Antonio, Robert J. 1981. Immanent Critique as the Core of Critical Theory: Its Origins and Developments in Hegel, Marx and Contemporary Thought. *British Journal of Sociology* 32, no. 3 (September): 330–345.

———. 1989. The Normative Foundations of Emancipatory Theory: Evolutionary versus Pragmatic Perspectives. *American Journal of Sociology* 94 (4): 721–748.

Antonio, Robert J., and Douglas Kellner. 1992. Communication, Modernity, and Democracy in Habermas and Dewey. *Symbolic Interaction* 15, no. 3 (Fall): 277–298.

Archer, Margaret. 1982. Morphogenesis versus Structuration: On Combining Structure and Action. *British Journal of Sociology* 33 (4): 455–483.

Aronowitz, Stanley. 2012. *Taking It Big: C. Wright Mills and the Making of Political Intellectuals.* New York: Columbia University Press.

Bacon, Michael. 2012. *Pragmatism: An Introduction.* Cambridge: Polity Press.

Baran, Paul A., and Paul M. Sweezy. 1968. *Monopoly Capital: An Essay on the American Economic and Social Order.* New York: Modern Reader Paperbacks.

Becker, Howard. 1999. The Chicago School, So-Called. *Qualitative Sociology* 22 (1): 3–12.

Bell, Wendell. 2008. *Foundations of Futures Studies: Values, Objectivity, and the Good Society.* New Brunswick, NJ: Transaction Publishers.

Berger, Peter L., and Thomas Luckman. 1967. *The Social Construction of Reality: A Treatise in the Sociology of Knowledge.* Garden City, NY: Anchor Books.

Bernstein, Richard. 1999. *Praxis and Action: Contemporary Philosophies of Human Action.* Philadelphia: University of Pennsylvania Press.

———. 2010. *The Pragmatic Turn.* Cambridge: Polity Press.

Bloor, David. 1997. *Wittgenstein, Rules and Institutions.* London: Routledge.

Blumer, Herbert. 1969. *Symbolic Interactionism: Perspective and Method.* Englewood Cliffs, NJ: Prentice Hall.

Bourdieu, Pierre. 1977. *Outline of a Theory of Practice.* Cambridge: Cambridge University Press.

Brinkmann, Svend. 2013. *John Dewey: Science for a Changing World.* New Brunswick, NJ: Transaction Publishers.

Burawoy, Michael. 2005a. Provincializing the Social Sciences. In *The Politics of Method in the Human Sciences: Positivism and Its Epistemological Others,* ed. George Steinmetz, 508–525. Durham, NC: Duke University Press.

———. 2005b. 2004 Presidential Address: For Public Sociology. *American Sociological Review* 70:4–28.

Dawe, Alan. 1970. The Two Sociologies. *British Journal of Sociology* 21 (2): 207–218.

Denzin, Norman K. 1992. *Symbolic Interactionism and Cultural Studies: The Politics of Interpretation.* Oxford: Blackwell Publishers.

Dewey, John. 1896. The Reflex Arc Concept in Psychology. *Psychological Review* 3:357–370.

———. 1934. *A Common Faith.* New Haven, CT: Yale University Press.

———. 1954. *The Public and Its Problems.* Chicago: Sage. First published 1927.

———. 1957. *Human Nature and Conduct.* New York: Modern Library. First published 1922.

———. 1958a. *Art as Experience.* New York: Capricorn Books. First published 1934.

———. 1958b. *Experience and Nature.* New York: Dover Publications. First published 1926.

———. 1960a. The Need for a Recovery of Philosophy. In *John Dewey: On Experience, Nature, and Freedom,* ed. Richard J. Bernstein, 19–69. Indianapolis: Bobbs-Merrill. First published in *Creative Intelligence: Essays in the Pragmatic Attitude,* 1917.

———. 1960b. *The Quest for Certainty.* New York: Capricorn Books. First published 1929.

———. 1963. *Freedom and Culture.* New York: Capricorn Books. First published 1939.

———. 1965. *The Influence of Darwin on Philosophy: And Other Essays in Contemporary Thought.* Bloomington: Indiana University Press. First Published 1910.

———.1966a. *Reconstruction in Philosophy.* Boston: Beacon Press. First published 1920.

———. 1966b. *Theory of Valuation.* Chicago: University of Chicago Press. First published 1939.

———. 2000. *Liberalism and Social Action.* Amherst, NY: Prometheus Books. First published 1935.

———. 2013. *Logic: The Theory of Inquiry.* Worcestershire, UK: Read Books. First published 1938.

Dewey, John, and Arthur Bentley. 1960. *Knowing and the Known.* Boston: Beacon Press. First published 1949.

Diggins, John Patrick. 1994. *The Promise of Pragmatism: Modernism and the Crisis of Knowledge and Authority.* Chicago: University of Chicago Press.

Dill, Jeffrey S. 2007. Durkheim and Dewey and the Challenge of Contemporary Moral Education. *Journal of Moral Education* 16, no. 2 (June): 221–237.

Dilthey, Wilhelm. 1961. *Pattern and Meaning in History: Thoughts on History and Society.* Ed. and intro. H. P. Rickman. New York: Harper Torchbooks.

Dunn, Robert G. 2008. *Identifying Consumption: Subjects and Objects in Consumer Society.* Philadelphia: Temple University Press.

Durkheim, Émile. 1951. *Suicide.* Glencoe, IL: Free Press.

———. 1956. *Education and Sociology.* Glencoe, IL: Free Press.

———. 1961. *Moral Education: A Study of the Theory and Application of the Sociology of Education.* Glencoe, IL: Free Press.

———. 1964. *The Division of Labor in Society.* New York: Free Press.

———. 1982. *The Rules of Sociological Method and Selected Texts on Sociology and Its Method.* Ed. Steven Lukes. New York: Free Press.

———. 1983. *Pragmatism and Sociology.* Cambridge: Cambridge University Press.

Featherstone, Joseph. 1972. Reconsideration: John Dewey. *New Republic,* July 8, 27–32.

Feuer, Lewis S., ed. 1959. *Marx and Engels: Basic Writings on Politics and Philosophy.* Garden City, NY: Anchor Books.

Fromm, Erich. 1941. *Escape from Freedom.* New York: Holt, Rinehart and Winston.

———. 1947. *Man for Himself: An Inquiry into the Psychology of Ethics.* Greenwich, CT: Fawcett Publications.

———. 1955. *The Sane Society.* New York: Rinehart.

Galbraith, John Kenneth. 1958. *The Affluent Society.* New York: Mentor Books.

Galgan, Jerald J. 1988. Marx and Dewey on the Unity of Theory and Practice. In *Context over Foundation,* ed. W. J. Gavin, 209–227. Dordrecht, Netherlands: D. Reidel Publishing.

Geary, Daniel. 2009. *Radical Ambition: C. Wright Mills, the Left, and American Social Thought.* Berkeley: University of California Press.

Gerth, Hans, and C. Wright Mills. 1964. *Character and Social Structure: The Psychology of Social Institutions.* New York: Harbinger. First published 1953.

Giddens, Anthony. 1979. *Central Problems in Social Theory: Action, Structure, and Contradiction in Social Analysis.* Berkeley: University of California Press.

———. 1984. *The Constitution of Society.* Berkeley: University of California Press.

Glaser, Barney, and Anselm Strauss. 2010. *The Discovery of Grounded Theory: Strategies for Qualitative Research.* New Brunswick, NJ: Aldine Transaction.

Goodman, Paul. 1956. *Growing Up Absurd: Problems of Youth in the Organized Society.* New York: Vintage Books.

Gorton, William A. 2010. The Philosophy of Social Science. In *Internet Encyclopedia of Philosophy.* Available at http://www.iep.utm.edu/soc-sci/.

Gouldner, Alvin W. 1962. Anti-Minotaur: The Myth of a Value-Free Sociology. *Social Problems* 9, no. 3 (Winter): 199–213.

———. 1970. *The Coming Crisis of Western Sociology.* New York: Basic Books.

Habermas, Jürgen. 1984. *The Theory of Communicative Action.* Vol. 1, *Reason and the Rationalization of Society.* Boston: Beacon Press.

Haney, David Paul. 2008. *The Americanization of Social Science: Intellectuals and Public Responsibility in the Postwar United States.* Philadelphia: Temple University Press.

Hays, Sharon. 1994. Structure and Agency and the Sticky Problem of Culture. *Sociological Theory* 12, no. 1 (March): 57–72.

Hook, Sydney. 1995. *John Dewey: An Intellectual Portrait.* Amherst, NY: Prometheus Press. First published 1939.

Horkheimer, Max, and Theodor W. Adorno. 1969. The Culture Industry: Enlightenment as Mass Deception. In *Dialectic of Enlightenment,* 120–167. New York: Seabury Press. First published 1944.

Horowitz, Irving Louis. 1983. *C. Wright Mills: An American Utopian.* New York: Free Press.

Jacobs, Jerry A. 2015. Top-Cited Articles in Sociology Journals, 2010–2014. *Footnotes* (American Sociological Association) 43, no. 8 (December): 9–10.

Jacoby, Russell. 1987. *The Last Intellectuals: American Culture in the Age of Academe.* New York: Basic Books.

James, William. 1955. *Pragmatism and Four Essays from* The Meaning of Truth. Cleveland: Meridian Books.

———. 1985. *The Varieties of Religious Experience: A Study in Human Nature.* New York: Penguin Books.

Jay, Martin. 1973. *The Dialectical Imagination: A History of the Frankfurt School and the Institute for Social Research 1923–1950.* Boston: Little, Brown.

———. 2005. *Songs of Experience: Modern American and European Variations on a Universal Theme.* Berkeley: University of California Press.

———. 2016. *Reason after Its Eclipse: On Late Critical Theory.* Madison: University of Wisconsin Press.

Joas, Hans. 1993. *Pragmatism and Social Theory.* Chicago: University of Chicago Press.

Kadlec, Alison. 2006. Reconstructing Dewey: The Philosophy of Critical Pragmatism. *Polity* 38, no. 4 (October): 520–542.

Kellner, Douglas. 1983. Critical Theory, Commodities, and the Consumer Society. *Theory, Culture, and Society* 1 (3): 66–83.

Lukacs, Georg. 1971. *History and Class Consciousness.* Cambridge, MA: MIT Press.

Lynd, Robert S. 1939. *Knowledge for What? The Place of Social Science in American Culture.* New York: Grove Press.

Lyotard, Jean-François. 1984. *The Postmodern Condition: A Report on Knowledge.* Minneapolis: University of Minnesota Press.

Mannheim, Karl. 1956. *Essays on the Sociology of Culture.* London: Routledge and Kegan Paul.

Marcuse, Herbert. 1964. *One Dimensional Man: Studies in the Ideology of Advanced Industrial Society.* Boston: Beacon Press.

Marx, Karl. 1906. *Capital: A Critique of Political Economy.* New York: Modern Library.

———. 1959. Manifesto of the Communist Party. In *Marx and Engels: Basic Writings on Politics and Philosophy.* Ed. Lewis S. Feuer. Garden City, NY: Doubleday/Anchor.

———. 1964. *Selected Writings in Sociology and Social Philosophy.* Trans. T. B. Bottomore. New York: McGraw-Hill.

Mead, George Herbert. 1956. *George Herbert Mead: On Social Psychology.* Ed. Anselm Strauss. Chicago: Phoenix Books. First published 1934.

———. 1980. *The Philosophy of the Present.* Ed. Arthur E. Murphy. Chicago: Phoenix Books. First published 1932.

Menand, Louis. 2001. *The Metaphysical Club: A Story of Ideas in America.* New York: Farrar, Straus and Giroux.

Merton, Robert K. 1957. *Social Theory and Social Structure.* Rev. and enl. ed. Glencoe, IL: Free Press.

Mills, C. Wright. 1956. *White Collar: The American Middle Classes.* New York: Oxford University Press/Galaxy. First published 1951.

———. 1958. The Man in the Middle: The Designer. *Industrial Design,* November.

———. 1959. *The Power Elite.* New York: Oxford University Press/Galaxy. First published 1956.

———. 1961. *The Sociological Imagination.* New York: Oxford University Press/Galaxy. First published 1959.

———. 1963a. Methodological Consequences of the Sociology of Knowledge. In *Power, Politics, and People: The Collected Essays of C. Wright Mills,* ed. Irving Louis Horowitz, 453–468. New York: Ballantine Books.

———. 1963b. *Power, Politics, and People: The Collected Essays of C. Wright Mills.* Ed. Irving Louis Horowitz. New York: Ballantine Books.

———. 1963c. The Professional Ideology of Social Pathologists. In *Power, Politics, and People: The Collected Essays of C. Wright Mills,* ed. Irving Louis Horowitz, 525–552. New York: Ballantine Books.

———. 1964. *Sociology and Pragmatism: The Higher Learning in America.* Ed. Irving Louis Horowitz. New York: Oxford University Press.

———. 2000. *C. Wright Mills: Letters and Autobiographical Writings.* Ed. Kathryn Mills and Pamela Mills. Berkeley: University of California Press.

———. 2008. *The Politics of Truth: Selected Writings of C. Wright Mills.* New York: Oxford University Press.

Morris, Aldon D. 2015. *The Scholar Denied: W.E.B. Du Bois and the Birth of Modern Sociology.* Berkeley: University of California Press.

Myrdal, Gunnar. 1969. *Objectivity in Social Research.* New York: Pantheon Books.

———. 2009. *An American Dilemma.* Vol. 1, *The Negro Problem and American Democracy.* New Brunswick, NJ: Transaction Publishers.

Ogburn, William F. 1966. *Social Change.* Oxford: Delta Books.

Packard, Vance. 1957. *The Hidden Persuaders.* New York: David McKay.

———. 1959. *The Status Seekers.* New York: David McKay.

———. 1960. *The Waste Makers.* Brooklyn: IG Publishing.

Pappas, Gregory F. 1998. Dewey's Ethics: Morality as Experience. In *Reading Dewey: Interpretations for a Postmodern Generation,* ed. Larry A. Hickman, 100–123. Bloomington: Indiana University Press.

Parsons, Talcott. 1951. *The Social System.* New York: Free Press.

Putnam, Hilary. 2002. *The Collapse of the Fact/Value Dichotomy and Other Essays.* Cambridge, MA: Harvard University Press.

Rabinow, Paul, and William M. Sullivan, eds. 1979. *Interpretive Social Science: A Reader.* Berkeley: University of California Press.

———. 1987. *Interpretive Social Science: A Second Look.* Berkeley: University of California Press.

Richardson, Robert D. 2006. *William James: In the Maelstrom of American Modernism.* Boston: Meridian Books.

Riesman, David. 1960. *Thorstein Veblen: A Critical Interpretation.* New York: Seabury Press.

———. 1993. *Abundance for What?* New York: Doubleday.

Riesman, David, with Nathan Glazer and Reuel Denny. 1961. *The Lonely Crowd.* New Haven, CT: Yale University Press. First published 1950.

Rosenberg, Bernard, and David Manning White, eds. 1957. *Mass Culture: The Popular Arts in America.* Glencoe, IL: Free Press.

Rytina, Joan Huber, and Charles P. Loomis. 1970. Marxist Dialectic and Pragmatism: Power as Knowledge. *American Sociological Review* 35 (April): 308–318.

Shalin, Dmitri N. 1992. Critical Theory and the Pragmatist Challenge. *American Journal of Sociology* 98, no. 2 (September): 237–279.

———. 1993. Modernity, Postmodernism, and Pragmatist Inquiry: An Introduction. *Symbolic Interaction* 16 (4): 303–332.

Shaw, Martin. 1973. The Coming Crisis in Radical Sociology. In *Ideology in Social Science: Readings in Critical Social Theory,* ed. Robin Blackburn, 32–44. New York: Vintage Books.

Simmel, Georg. 1990. *The Philosophy of Money.* Ed. David Frisby. London: Routledge.

Slater, Philip. 1970. *The Pursuit of Loneliness: American Culture at the Breaking Point.* Boston: Beacon Press.

Sluga, Hans. 2014. *Politics and the Search for the Common Good.* Cambridge: Cambridge University Press.

Stahl, Titus. 2014. What Is Immanent Critique? *Social Science Research News,* June 3, 1–20.

Steinmetz, George, ed. 2005. *The Politics of Method in the Human Sciences: Positivism and Its Epistemological Others.* Durham, NC: Duke University Press.

Stone, Gregory P., and Harvey A. Farberman. 1967. On the Edge of Rapprochement: Was Durkheim Moving toward the Perspective of Symbolic Interaction? *Sociological Quarterly* 8 (Spring): 149–164.

Streeten, Paul. 1958. Introduction. In *Value in Social Theory,* by Gunnar Myrdal. Ed. Paul Streeten. New York: Harper and Brothers.

Talisse, Robert B., and Scott F. Aiken. 2008. *Pragmatism: A Guide for the Perplexed.* London: Continuum International Publishing.

Tawney, R. H. 1948. *The Acquisitive Society.* New York: Harvest.

Tenbruck, F. H. 1965. Formal Sociology. *Essays on Sociology, Philosophy, and Aesthetics by Georg Simmel et al.*, ed. Kurt H. Wolff, 61–99. New York: Harper Torchbook.

Tilman, Rick. 1984. *C. Wright Mills: A Native Radical and his American Intellectual Roots.* University Park: Pennsylvania State University Press.

———. 2004. *Thorstein Veblen, John Dewey, C. Wright Mills, and the Generic Ends of Life.* London: Rowman and Littlefield.

Tucker, Kenneth H., Jr. 1998. *Anthony Giddens and Modern Social Theory.* London: Sage.

Veblen, Thorstein. 1934. *The Theory of the Leisure Class: An Economic Study of Institutions.* New York: Modern Library.

Weber, Max. 1947. The Fundamental Concepts of Sociology. In *Max Weber: The Theory of Social and Economic Organization,* ed. Talcott Parsons and A. M. Henderson, 87–157. Glencoe, IL: Free Press.

———. 1949. "Objectivity" in Social Science and Social Policy. In *The Methodology of the Social Sciences,* by Max Weber. New York: Free Press.

———. 1958a. *The Protestant Ethic and the Spirit of Capitalism.* New York: Charles Scribner's Sons.

———. 1958b. Religious Rejections of the World and Their Directions. In *From Max Weber: Essays in Sociology,* ed. H. H. Gerth and C. Wright Mills, 323–359. New York: Oxford University Press/Galaxy.

———. 1958c. Science as a Vocation. In *From Max Weber: Essays in Sociology,* ed. H. H. Gerth and C. Wright Mills, 129–156. New York: Oxford University Press/Galaxy.

West, Cornell. 1989. *The American Evasion of Philosophy: A Genealogy of Pragmatism.* Madison: University of Wisconsin Press.

White, Morton. 1947. *Social Thought in America: The Revolt against Formalism.* Boston: Beacon Press.

Whitehead, Alfred North. 1958. *Science and the Modern World.* New York: Mentor Books. First published 1925.

Whyte, William H. 1956. *The Organization Man.* New York: Simon and Schuster.

Wiley, Norbert. 1979. The Rise and Fall of Dominating Theories in American Sociology. In *Contemporary Issues in Theory and Research,* ed. William E. Snizek, Ellsworth R. Fuhrman, and Michael K. Miller, 47–79. Westport, CT: Greenwood Press.

Wittgenstein, Ludwig. 2009. *Philosophical Investigations.* Hoboken, NJ: Wiley-Blackwell.

Index

Robert G. Dunn is Professor Emeritus of Sociology, California State University, East Bay. He is the author of *Identifying Consumption: Subjects and Objects in Consumer Society* (Temple) and *Identity Crises: A Social Critique of Postmodernity.*